BIRDHOUSES

BIRDHOUSES

*A Step-By-Step Guide to Building Attractive Homes
For Your Feathered Friends*

JOHN KELSEY

PRC

First published in 2002 by
PRC Publishing Ltd,
64 Brewery Road, London N7 9NT

A member of **Chrysalis** Books plc

Distributed in the U.S. and Canada by:
Sterling Publishing Co., Inc.
387 Park Avenue South
New York, NY 10016

ISBN 1 85648 649-4

Printed and bound in China

ACKNOWLEDGMENTS

The publisher wishes to thank John Kelsey for providing all the photography and illustrations in
this book, including the front and back cover photography, with the following exceptions:

Page 6 courtesy of © Cheryl A. Ertelt/RSPCA Photolibrary;
Pages 7 (top), 8 (top) and 9 courtesy of © Mike Lane/RSPCA Photolibrary;
Page 7 (bottom) courtesy of © George McCarthy/Wild Images/RSPCA Photolibrary;
Page 8 (bottom) courtesy of © Richard Mittleman/RSPCA Photolibrary.

Contents

Introduction

Making a birdhouse for bluebirds is a popular choice as it offers a viable alternative for their threatened natural woodland habitat.

Nest boxes come in many shapes and sizes and choosing which design to build will mostly depend on which species you want to attract, where you plan to locate the box, and what type of area you live in. The projects shown in the book show a wide variety of designs and ways to make birdhouses for those new to carpentry, as well as more experienced woodworkers. Look at all the projects first before deciding which one is best for you.

A nest box should be well constructed, durable, easy to check and clean, and, most of all, built with its purpose in mind. A birdhouse that is built for decorative rather than practical purposes probably won't entice birds to move in. Some of the boxes in this book are painted, but generally it is best to use untreated wood such as pine, cedar, or fir, with the walls being at least ¾in (20mm) thick. If you do want to paint your box then it's best to only paint the outside.

Boxes should have rough interiors for fledglings to cling onto (this enables them to move around), drainage holes to keep the interior dry, ventilation for air, and easy access for cleaning once the young birds have flown the nest. A good birdhouse must be securely mounted and also provide the occupants with protection from predators. When placing your birdhouse it is best to avoid areas where pesticides and herbicides are used, as chemicals may decrease and sometimes eliminate insect populations—the primary food source for birds.

Make and place your birdhouse before the breeding season begins and don't be discouraged if the birds do not nest immediately; sometimes it takes a while for them to find their lovingly created new home. The types of birds that will be attracted to your birdhouse will depend on the habitat surrounding your box and the design of the box itself (see the chart in the Birdhouse Woodworking chapter for the dimensions that each species likes). Nest boxes for bluebirds, for example, should be placed in open habitat, while robins and starlings prefer boxes high up on the wall of a building, and martins like their houses to be 15ft (4.5m) to 20ft (6m) in the air. You will often find robin and starling nests high in the eaves of old farm buildings, or on top of the exposed roof beams of a contemporary house. Purple martins like an apartment block type of birdhouse with space for six or eight martin pairs in each layer, or they will also occupy a cluster of high-rise towers (see page 118).

Some of the bigger projects in this book might look rather complicated to build, but don't be put off, they're just a stack of basic roof-style birdhouses. And they're worth the effort; it's wonderful to have a flock rather than a single pair nesting in your backyard. Bluebird houses are a favorite as the birds are so beautiful and because these houses provide a replacement for their decreasing natural woodland habitat. The Peterson style of house for bluebirds (see page 84) tapers inside to a small floor, so it more closely resembles a natural cavity in a tree

Above: To attract the nuthatch and hear its wonderful song construct a birdhouse with an entrance hole $1\frac{1}{4}$ to $1\frac{1}{3}$in (30 to 35mm) in diameter.

Left: A pair of red-bellied woodpecker at a nest box.

trunk. Its oval-shaped entry is also more like a natural opening, making bluebirds feel more at home. Woodpeckers seem to like a tall box, such as the plug birdhouse, and the rougher the wood, the better. The best type of wood to use for this type of box is log-sawn cedar fencing, rough-sawn flat on one side, with the bark left on the other side.

If you want to attract a variety of species and have ample room, you may consider pairing your boxes. You can place them on poles 15 to 25ft (4.5 to 7.5m) apart or even back to back.

House sparrows don't need much help when it comes to their accommodation, but they will often be seen on a well-stocked bird table.

Birds such as tree swallows and bluebirds will nest closely to one another, though not all species are as accommodating.

No birdhouse book would be complete without a feeder. The one included shown on page 104 is a hexagonal shape that is surprisingly easy to make, as well as being an attractive design. Hang it by light chains from a tree branch or an overhanging eave and fill it through the hole in the top, before plugging it with the cap.

Common predators of nest boxes include raccoons, snakes, cats, and squirrels. But don't despair, it is fairly easy to thwart their activities. Some of the projects in this book, such as the basic birdhouse (page 38), have a double-thick plate that surrounds the entrance hole, so cats and raccoons cannot reach their paws inside. A raccoon is clever enough to open a regular hook-and-eye, so use a wire twist-tie through a pair of screw-eyes to keep a birdhouse closed to his attentions, as shown in the bluebird house project. The twist-tie is beyond a raccoon's ability, but easy for you to open so you can inspect the nestlings.

Cats are difficult to deter because of their cunning ability to get into things you don't want them to. They may look cute and cuddly, but once cats learn bird boxes are a good source of food they'll leap to the top of the box and dip into the entrance hole with their paws to grab at the contents. To counter this a cat proof bird box is included in this book (page 72). The extended front of this nest box is almost impossible

Tree swallows prefer open areas, so position the birdhouse on a post near a tree or fence. They will lay about four to seven eggs.

A robin enjoys a meal from a garden food tray.

for a cat to climb over. With a double thickness of wood at the opening, a locking catch, and the box mounted on a smooth metal pole, this little fortress is all but impregnable to cats.

It is not a good idea to include outside perches on the birdhouse, because the birds that use them can be a nuisance rather than the birds you wish to attract. Perches might also help other predators gain access. A smooth metal pipe is also a cunning foil as predators find them difficult to climb. For additional protection against predators an overhanging roof is also a good feature, and this can be seen in the box birdhouse project.

Once you have gone to the effort of building your nest box, you will need to maintain it. Before the nesting season begins, repair any damaged ones, or replace them all together. They also need to be cleaned before each season in order to attract more feathered friends to use your well-crafted facilities. You could make the roof of a birdhouse removable for cleaning, as shown in the roof birdhouse project on page 46. Alternatively, you could nail the roof to the back and sides, and hinge the front to the floor, or make a toggle floor, as shown in the basic birdhouse project. Whatever design you decide to use, you are sure to be inspired and will enjoy several months of birdwatching during the breeding season.

Birdhouse Woodworking

A birdhouse can be anything you want, so long as you don't really expect any birds to move in. It can be fanciful, colorful, and placed artistically in the landscape. A nest box, on the other hand, provides much-needed housing for cavity-nesting birds, who every year lose more habitat to urbanization. A nest box has to meet a list of requirements (page 38) or the birds won't move in.

It is possible to build attractive and interesting birdhouses that will also work as nest boxes and this applies to the houses in this book. There are certain things you need to do such as locating them appropriately in the birds' habitat and guarding them against cats and other predators.

The best thing about making birdhouses is their scale and their scope as projects. The largest apartment house for purple martins can be built in a weekend, and most nest boxes can be completed in a pleasant evening. Suitable materials, such as soft woods including cedar, fir, and pine, are readily available and easy to work. In the bygone age when middle schools taught woodshop and boy scouts earned merit badges for making shavings, a birdhouse was often an early project. For woodworking beginners, that is still true. A birdhouse is a great way to learn about tools and materials, and to practice basic skills. Mistakes don't cost much and success can come quickly.

Materials for birdhouses

Bird experts agree that the best material for nest boxes is softwood about ¾in (19mm or 20mm) thick. In North America this is sold as 1 x (one-by) lumber, as in 1 x 4, 1 x 6, 1 x 8, and 1 x 10. Thinner material can't withstand the weather. Rough lumber is a better choice than smooth. Paint and wood preservatives can poison the birds, so should be avoided; if you must paint, use artist's acrylic or exterior latex, and only paint the outside of the house. There's some evidence that birdhouses painted white on the outside are cooler inside than houses left unpainted. However there's no evidence one way or the other about what the birds prefer—perhaps they enjoy a sauna.

Ordinary pine lumber is good for birdhouses. It starts out a light yellow in color but soon weathers to gray. Cedar siding is attractive, durable, weather-resistant, easy to work, inexpensive, and also weathers to gray. Visit a full-service lumber yard, the kind of place that caters to carpenters and building contractors, and browse their selection of softwoods and solid-wood siding materials. In New England, the offerings commonly include No. 2 Western pine S2S (surfaced two sides), and S1S (surfaced one side) cedar, No. 3 grade, which is used for most of the houses in this book. This material has square edges, with one rough side and one side planed smooth. Some siding has machined or molded edges so it fits attractively together. Some birdhouse designs can use it as is, and if molded siding is all you can find don't fret because you can always saw the moldings off.

Novice woodworkers may feel cheated when measuring what's sold as 1 x 6 or 1 x 8. The 1 x 6 actually measures about ¾in (19mm) thick, by 5½in (140mm) wide and the 1 x 8 is only 7¼in (185mm) wide. The reason for this is that the board was as big as its nominal size when they sawed it out of the log. Subsequent drying and machining made it smaller, so you are paying for what they started with.

While you are browsing the lumber yard, look at the wooden roofing materials. You may find red cedar barn shakes, which are between ⅜in (9mm) and ½in (12mm) thick, 18in (450mm) long, and variable in width from about 3in (75mm) to 12in (300mm). They are called shakes because they have been split out of the log, not sawn. They are attractive, easy to work, and excellent for birdhouse roofs. You may

1
Softwood lumber: Birdhouses can make good use of short ends of wood, rough wood, and the less expensive grades of wood. To tell whether a board is straight, look along its edge.

2
One-by: This stack is No. 3 cedar siding which is rough on one side, ideal for birdhouses. From the bottom up the sizes are: 1 x 10, 1 x 8, 1 x 6, 1 x 4, and 1 x 2.

3
Siding nails: Look for special nails manufactured for attaching wood siding to houses. They're galvanized, so they don't rust, and thinner than construction nails, so they're less likely to split the wood.

4
Roofing: Cedar barn shakes, which have rough surfaces because they were split out of the log, make excellent roofing material for birdhouses. Barn shakes are about 18in (450mm) long, ⅜in (9mm) to ½in (12mm) thick, and random in width.

also find sawn shingles, which taper in thickness from one end to the other, and sawn clapboard in various widths. Shakes, shingles, and clapboards come in bundles. Lumber yards usually won't split a bundle, but sometimes one has come apart on its own and, since builders will not take it, you can get a deal on an armload of really good birdhouse material.

Look for nails that are specifically sold for shingles, siding, and shakes. They'll be galvanized to resist rust, and thin but somewhat rough so they sink in without splitting the wood and resist coming out. As to length, select ones that are 1½in (37mm), 2in (50mm), and 2½in (60mm or 65mm) long. If you prefer to work with screws instead of nails, choose No. 6 or No. 8 galvanized screws sold for outdoor construction. Don't use black drywall screws or interior screws because they will rust. Select the same lengths as nails, that is, 1¼in (30mm), 1⅝in (40mm), and 2in (50mm).

If you live in the country you might have access to used wood from abandoned outbuildings, which can be perfect for birdhouses. If you are harvesting this material yourself, be sure to wear gloves and heavy boots. Pull all the nails first, preferably on site before you carry any of the wood away. Set up on a pair of sawhorses with a hammer, pry-bar, and vise-grip pliers. Make sure you are thorough and methodical by pulling all the nails, chucking them in a box or tin can, and disposing of them all at once. If you don't, you are almost certain to jam a rusty nail into your hand or foot and acquire a nasty puncture wound, usually followed by another painful jab—your overdue tetanus booster shot.

Without getting too far into wood technology, it is important to understand the difference between wood, which is a non-uniform formerly living material, and plastic, which solidifies from a liquid and is the same in all directions. Wood is made of fibers and has an internal structure, or grain. Like the head of a broom, the fibers in a piece of wood all run in one direction. Consequently you can cut or split wood with the grain, that is in the direction of the fibers, whereas you can saw or cut wood across the grain but you cannot split it. Woodworking saws and drills are designed with this in mind. The teeth of some tools cut better across the grain, which is called crosscutting, and some cut better with the grain, which is known as ripping.

For indoor applications, woodworkers also need to understand wood movement. All wood, whether coated with a finish or not, absorbs or releases water vapor until it reaches equilibrium with the moisture content of the atmosphere. The wood also shrinks and expands along with its changing moisture content—a piece of wood is bigger when it is wet than when it is dry. The tricky part is, the change in dimension occurs in both width and thickness, that is, across the fibers, but not in length. Since heated indoor air is a lot dryer than outdoor air, wood movement can be a big deal when you bring boards indoors from outdoor storage. This isn't a problem with birdhouses as they stay outdoors and aren't very big, so there is less worry about wood movement.

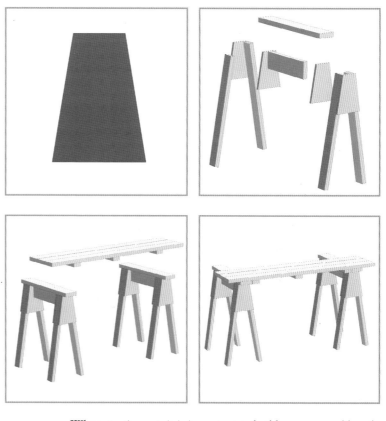

When starting out, it is important to build a secure workbench.

Workshop

Whether you are going to make birdhouses or bureaus, you need a bench on which to work. It can be as simple as planks nailed across a pair of sawhorses. But it must be sturdy enough to withstand hammering and sawing, without wobbling around.

The workbench used in this book is a heavy beam made from two 4 x 6 timbers, resting across a pair of trestles. The workshop is equally simple—a one-car garage bay, with the bench in the middle and tool cabinets and shelves lined solidly along one side and end. There is enough storage to put everything away, so the bench can be completely clear for working. The storage wall includes a rolling tool cabinet with a flat top, kept clear for the tools needed by any current project. There is also a small bench fastened to the wall, for use as an assembly table and parts-staging area.

If you are just starting out and you don't have a bench or worktable, the simplest remedy would be two or three 6ft (2m) 2 x 8 planks butted together edge-to-edge and

Beam
1½ x 3½ x 24in
(37 x 90 x 600mm)

Rail
1½ x 3½ x 12in
(37 x 90 x 300mm)

Bench Top
1½ x 17 x 72in
(37 x 430 x 1800mm)
Make from three 2 x 6
planks.

Cleat
1½ x 3½ x 16in
(37 x 90 x 400)

Leg
Make from 1 x 4 or 2 x 4
Leg length = horse
height including top

Brace
¾ x 9¼ x 12in
(20 x 235 x 300mm)

75 degrees

Join the parts with glue and galvanized screws.

Portable Sawhorse Workbench

screwed to a batten, resting on a pair of sawhorses. Hardware stores sell metal brackets for making sawhorses out of construction lumber; you can make your own following the drawing shown opposite. Arrange the planks across the horses so they overhang about an inch on one side, which is the side where you will stand to work. Join them together by gluing and screwing two or three 2 x 4 battens underneath. Then position the sawhorses so the battens stop against them. For more stability, screw the top to the sawhorses. The correct height of the bench depends on your own height—stand up straight, arms at your sides, and hold one hand out flat, palm facing the floor. If you had a workbench, your palm would be resting on its surface, and that is about the right height for you. For example, your author, who is 5ft 9in (1.75m) tall, has a bench with a top 34in (86cm) off the floor.

People commonly begin woodworking in a garage. However, if you or your spouse insists upon actually parking a car in your workshop, consider taking over the basement, the family room, a spare bedroom, or a covered deck or patio. The workshop really needs to be a dedicated space. Along with room to work and storage for tools and hardware, you will need space for new and surplus materials, as well as for your inevitable collection of incomplete projects.

Tools and Techniques

You can build a very elaborate birdhouse with a basic kit of tools. The same tools will help you through most household repairs and many small construction projects. When buying tools, you generally can expect to get what you pay for, sometimes less but never more. While you don't need the most expensive professional tools, the cheapest tools are no bargain because either they won't do the job at all, or if they do work, they won't last. The frustrations caused by cheap tools can take all the pleasure out of woodworking.

Most woodworking projects follow the same basic series of eight steps. The details depend on what tools you have and what techniques you have learned for using them. The basic sequence of steps is:

Step one: Choose your project and study the working drawings, or draw your own plans, to describe the idea you have in mind.

5
Basic workbench: Your workbench has to be sturdy, flat, and at the right height for your body. This 8ft (2.4m) bench has a heavy top made by gluing two 4 x 6 beams together. The top rests across a pair of sawhorse-like trestles. The 4 x 4 back support and 1 x 12 tool tray are handy optional details. Gravity holds this bench together—it can come apart in a minute if used in a garage and you want to make room for a car. There is a vise at one end of the bench, plus another vise on the assembly table in the background, but these aren't necessary for any projects shown here.
6
Sawhorse bench: Here's the sawhorse-style of portable workbench shown in the drawings on pages 13 and 14, outdoors on a fine spring day.

7
A few good clamps: A small investment in clamps gives you the huge advantage of extra hands. The red-handled quickset clamps have 6in (150mm), 8in (200mm), and 12in (300mm) bars. The orange-handled spring clamps exert a surprising amount of pressure.

8
Clamp for safety: Use clamps to hold the work on the bench, so you can concentrate on sawing or drilling. The clamp not only keeps the workpiece from swinging around, it also keeps your hands away from the cutting action.

9
Clamp to test fit: Use clamps to see how parts and subassemblies are going to fit together. You can see what is the wrong size and fix it. To set a clamp like this, first plant the fixed jaw on the work and hold it in position with one hand, and use the other hand to position and tighten the movable jaw.

10
Clamp to glue: Use clamps to hold parts together while you drive nails or screws, and while glued assemblies dry.

Step two: List the materials you will need, and obtain them. Most of the plans in this book include a bill of materials and a parts-cutting diagram.

Step three: Mark parts to length and width and saw them out. Sawing a piece of wood so it is the size you want, and still has nice, square sides and ends, is the most fundamental set of woodworking skills (see page 18).

Step four: Drill holes, make grooves and other details as needed.

Step five: Nail or screw individual parts into subassemblies, for example, attach birdhouse sides to floor. Combine subassemblies and remaining loose parts, for example, roof pieces to birdbox.

Step six: Add hinges, latches, mounting bolts, and other hardware.

Step seven: Apply finish, if any.

Step eight: Install.

Holding the work

Clamps are your third hand. Use them to hold subassemblies together while you drive screws or nails, or to hold wood down safely on the workbench, while you saw it or drill it. Clamps not only help you achieve accurate work, they are important safety devices.

How do clamps keep you safe? Most injuries from hand tools and portable power tools, such as drills and jigsaws, occur when trying to hold the work with one hand, and driving the tool with the other hand. The driving hand is not strong and steady enough, so the tool slips. Where does it go? It slices or saws or pokes or mashes into the holding hand. This kind of hand injury is almost inevitable whenever you try to hand-hold the workpiece, but is entirely avoidable once you learn to use clamps effectively.

Use clamps to hold the workpiece tightly onto the workbench or sawhorse as they are much stronger than you are and don't bleed when things go wrong. Things are less likely to go awry when you have got two hands available for bracing and guiding the tool into a workpiece that can't move around. For work on the scale of birdhouses, you need four 12in (30cm) clamps, plus four spring-style clamps but the more the better.

Measuring and layout tools

You cannot buy materials, or measure anything bigger than 12in (30cm), without a tape measure. There are many sizes; choose a 25ft (8m) tape that is 1in (25mm) wide. Use a speed square or try square to draw a line that is 90 degrees, or square, to the edge of the wood. Use a compass for drawing circles and stepping off distances. Make lines on the wood with a medium-black pencil. Pencil marks can seen, and can be erased.

11
Measure and mark: These basic measuring and layout tools include an inexpensive vernier caliper, which measures thickness and distance to $\frac{1}{128}$in (.2mm); 25ft (8m) tape measure; 6in (150mm) try square; sharp pencil, and carpenter's speed square, which contains a protractor for measuring angles.

12
Miscellaneous tools: You'll find all of these tools to be useful additions to your kit. The needle-nosed vise-grip pliers (top) can grab almost anything. From left: nail-pulling pliers, screw-starting awl, center-finding awl, nailset, sharp little knife, and wide chisel.

13 & 14
Crosscut: Sawing wood to length is crosscutting across the grain. Square a layout line across the wood, clamp it to the bench so the sawing line is over the edge, and drive the saw along the line. Avoid a splintered end by catching the so-called falling board before it falls.

Cutting wood to length and width

The birdhouses and nest boxes in this book mostly use standard widths of lumber, so most of the sawing is crosscutting, to make the pieces the correct length. You can do all of it with a hand-saw; you can mechanize for not much money with a portable electric jigsaw, or you can go all the way with a table saw or a chop saw.

Stanley and its competitors currently make a series of short, sharp handsaws with teeth patterned after Japanese saws. These are a very effective and affordable tool. If you can, buy two: one coarse, about 6 to 8 teeth per inch, and one fine, 12 to 15 teeth per inch.

If you want to step up to a power saw, a portable jigsaw would be the place to start. It will saw straight lines and curves, and it can accept special blades for sawing such materials as aluminum and plywood. For solid wood, choose a coarse blade, 6 to 8 teeth per inch.

Though a table saw is standard in woodworking shops, many skilled homeowners and professional finish carpenters alike prefer a motorized miter saw, or chop saw. These machines have been redesigned over the past ten years. Current models are extremely accurate, rugged, and well-guarded. The sliding-arm version can handle material a foot or more in width. Picture 17 shows a miter-saw setup, but choosing

15
Rip: Sawing the wood to width is ripping with the grain. Make the setup so you won't accidentally saw into the bench, the clamp, or the saw's power cord.

16
Saws: The portable electric jigsaw is an extremely versatile tool that can saw accurately enough for birdhouse projects. The short toolbox saw in the center is the muscle-powered equivalent. The English dovetail saw at the top has a thin blade with a spine for stiffness; it cuts on the push stroke. The Japanese dozuki saw in the foreground cuts on the pull stroke. Either one of these will make fine and accurate cuts.

17
Jigsaw: A portable electric jigsaw will handle nearly all birdhouse-scale sawing tasks. A saw like this can accept a variety of blades for different materials, and its stroke can be adjusted to suit different materials, and its sole tilts for making angled cuts.

18
Chop saw: A sliding-arm miter saw, or chop saw, makes extremely accurate crosscuts and bevel cuts in material up to 12in (300mm) wide. This one is built into its own bench, which supports long boards as they are being sawn.

and learning how to use a miter saw or a table saw is beyond the scope of this book.

Cabinetmakers cut delicate little parts and make intricate joints with a small, sharp back-saw. The European version of this tool is the dovetail saw; the Japanese version is the dozuki (see picture 16, page 18); the low-cost hobby version is the X-Acto disposable-blade saw. Any of these saws will make a small, straight cut with or across the grain of the wood.

Drilling holes of all sizes

Drill holes for the bird entrance, for ventilation and for screws. The old tool for drilling holes in wood is a brace and bit, a muscle-powered weapon that also can be used to drive screws. The contemporary tool is an electric drill powered by a rechargeable battery. Today's rechargeable battery models are tough and reliable. You won't have any down time if you keep two batteries, one in the charger and one in the drill. Drills are sold by maximum chuck size; ⅜in (9mm) is a suitable size.

You will see both approaches in this book. An electric drill does nothing that a brace can't match and if you were to decide there was high virtue in working entirely with hand tools, then by all means go ahead. You can buy an excellent used brace at a flea market for about $10; a new one can cost up to $100.

19
Brace and bit: The old-fashioned brace is excellent for making bird-entry holes using an adjustable expansion bit. The workpiece is securely clamped to the bench on top of a protective piece of wood.

20
Extra leverage: When the hole is large, you might need more traction. You can clamp the workpiece so it's vertical and lean into it, or you can apply your body weight by getting right on top of it.

21
Hole saw: A plumber's hole saw driven by an electric drill can make a clean hole in no time. The workpiece is clamped to the bench atop a protective piece of scrap, allowing you to grab the drill with both hands and tuck it into your body. A plastic face shield is comfortable to wear, so it is easy insurance against a stray chip in the eye.

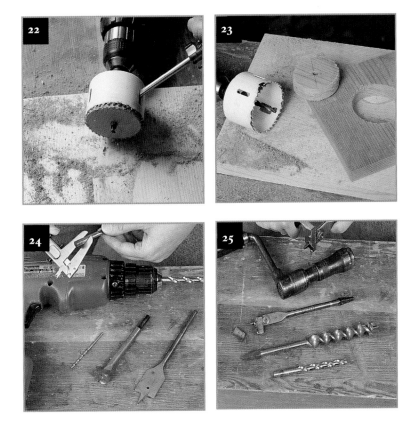

22 & 23
A neat disk: Unlike a regular drill bit, which makes only chips, the hole saw creates a waste disk of wood, which you might be able to use for something else. Pry it out of the saw with a screwdriver.

24
Power drill: Here is a collection of typical bits for electric drills. These include twist drill bits (which can also be used in a hand-powered brace), Powerbore bits and spade bits. The vernier caliper confirms the size of a twist bit.

25
Muscle power: Here are typical bits for use with the brace. The expansion bit, center and top, adjusts in size by turning a screw set into its back side. The auger bit in the center has two cutting lips. The twist bit in the foreground can also be used in an electric drill.

The cutting tools that a drill uses are called bits. Except in small sizes, bits made to be used with a brace cannot be swapped into an electric drill, and vice versa. However, they are interchangeable up to a certain size in diameter—you can use a standard twist drill bit (like the ones shown in picture 24) in wood, metal, and plastic, powered by hand or by machine. Unless you are prepared to learn the intricacies of sharpening drill bits, you should buy new ones as you need them, and avoid sets that are used.

To make holes up to about 1in (25mm) in diameter with a brace and bit, you will need a set of auger bits. These have a screw point to help them draw into the wood, one or two spurs to score the wood fibers and cut across them, and one or two cutting lips to form and lift the chips out of the hole. For larger holes, up to about 3in (75mm), you will need an expansion bit (like the one shown in picture 25). It has the same screw point as a regular auger bit, but the spur and cutting lip slide in a groove so they can be set to almost any size.

To make holes up to about 1in (25mm) in diameter with an electric drill, most woodworkers would use a spade bit. These have a triangular point that leads into the wood, and a pair of cutting lips that scrape and lift the chips. For larger holes, up to about 3in (75mm) in diameter, use a hole saw (like the one shown in picture 21, page 19). Some hole-saw systems fit a variety of sawing heads onto a common mandrel and center drill, while other systems are complete at each diameter with no interchangeable parts. Hole saws are expensive, so unless you also do residential plumbing, which requires feeding pipes through joists and studs, start with only the sizes you actually need and add new ones as you need them.

Drills work off the center of the hole, so measure and mark on the wood to locate that. Always clamp the workpiece on top of a protective piece of scrap wood. Drill in easy bites, frequently lifting the bit out of the work to clear the chips. Otherwise the chips will interfere with the cutting action and cause frictional heat that not only scorches the wood, but may also destroy the drill bit.

It is often tempting to hand hold the workpiece for drilling, but if you do that, you are almost certain to injure yourself. Whether your drill is powered by muscle or by electricity, you need two hands to drive it and guide it, and you do not need any hands in the path of a cutting tool that easily can slip, or a workpiece that can get caught and start to spin around. You must clamp the workpiece every time.

What can you do if you drill the wrong size hole? If it is a birdhouse entry, no problem: just add a protective entry plate with the right-sized hole. But if it is too small, you can drill it to make it larger, provided you can temporarily fill it in to provide a center for the drill bit. (See page 22 for how to do this.)

26

Hit it: The household curved-claw hammers with gray handles (right and center) have a 16-ounce head, and most people will be comfortable swinging them. Small people probably will be more comfortable with the red-handled cabinetmaker's hammer (top), or the small Japanese hammer (left), each weighing about 10 ounces.

Hammers

The hammer is the oldest tool and hammers come in almost infinite variety. The one you need, however, is a standard household hammer with a curved claw. A carpenter's framing hammer looks almost the same, except its nail-pulling claw is straight, and it is probably a lot heavier.

If you follow the basic construction methods presented in this book, you will be driving a lot of nails. It will be important to find a hammer that suits your body size and arm strength. One of the people who built birdhouses for this book is a small woman with tiny hands. She does not have the arm strength to swing a full-size 16 ounce carpenter's hammer, but she does very well indeed with a 10 ounce hammer.

Redrilling holes to be larger

1 & 2

Plug it: Before you can redrill a hole that is too small, you have to fill it in so the drill center has a place to bite. Cut a square plug sized so you have to hammer it into the hole. You want the corners to dig into the surrounding wood so the plug stays put.

3 & 4

Drill it: The adjustable bit in the hand-powered brace can be set to almost any size. Its threaded tip will pull it into the wood of the plug that was driven into the too-small hole, then its cutting spurs will chew through the plug and the surrounding wood.

5

Clean it up: The plug drops out as you reach the bottom of the hole, leaving a little ring of wood to be cut away. Go at it with a sharp knife.

How to drive nails

Everybody knows how to drive a nail and you have probably already mastered the necessary skills. However if you are unhappy with your results, try the following basic method. The steps are:

- Dry-fit the two pieces together so you are sure how they go, and draw a layout line on which you intend to place the nails. Make a little cross where each nail will go. Normally two or three nails will be plenty; if there is any doubt add glue, not more nails.

- Lay the first workpiece flat on the bench and start all the nails. Drive all of them almost through the wood, and drive one of them a dab farther so it just begins to come through the other side.

- Fit the two pieces back together and press the single protruding nail into the second piece of wood to help hold it in position. In many situations it will help a lot if you now clamp the two pieces together.

- With the assembly resting firmly on the bench, drive the first nail down to the surface of the wood. Hold the hammer by the handle, not the shank; lock your wrist and swing from the elbow for control or from the shoulder for power. If the nail begins to bend or to lean sideways, then don't try to

27
Layout line: Nailing always goes better when you make a layout line showing where the nails ought to be. Here the middle finger bearing against the edge of the wood acts as a gauge for drawing a line that is straight enough.
28
Start flat: To start the nails, plant the workpiece flat on the bench. Drive the nails so they don't quite come through the other side.
29 & 30
Starter nail: Drive one nail a little farther than the others, so its point just comes through the other side. When you align the pieces to be joined, press the starter nail into the wood. It will help keep everything in place while you hammer it home.

Common nailing problems and how to correct them.

1
Triple oops: Some days everything goes wrong. The nail on the left went into a knot and started to bend. The middle nail hit a twist in the wood grain and came out through the side. The nail on the right is not going anywhere, even though it is on the layout line.

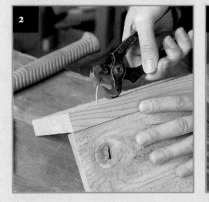

2 & 3
Pull them out: Use the pliers, or the vise grips, to lever the offending nails out of the wood. Protect the surface of the wood with a thin scrap. Do not try to straighten and reuse bent nails.

4
Drive them out: This nail came out through the side as it was being driven home, now there is no opening for the pliers under the nail head. Turn the workpiece over on the edge of the bench and use a nail set to tap the nail point back the way it came. Drive it just far enough to get a grip with the pliers or the hammer claw.

correct it—pull it out and start again nearby with a new nail. If you are new to this, sink a few into scrap wood for practice.

- Look and feel to check the position and alignment of the two pieces of wood, and adjust as necessary. A sharp tap with the hammer will shift the wood even though the first nail has gone home. Drive the second and third nails.

How to drive screws

Screws hold so powerfully that they are overkill to use for birdhouses, but many people find them easier to manage than nails. People who have not grown up with hammers in their hands often have trouble driving nails. They bend, they go crooked, they come out through the edge, the hammer slips and dings the wood. In nearly every situation you could use screws instead. Even though in soft woods such as cedar you can get away without pilot holes, you will always get a neater job if you take the time to drill them. Here is the sequence to follow:

- Dry-fit the two pieces together so you are sure how they go, and draw a layout line in pencil on which you intend to place the screws. Mark where each screw will go. Normally two or three screws will be plenty.
- Clamp the pieces together and if you can, clamp the whole assembly to the bench or trap it in the vise. Start the clamp, tap the

31
Pilot holes: These bits make pilot holes for screws. Although their length is adjustable, you do need to match the bit diameter to the screw size.

32
Driver tips: These screwdriver bits can be used with a power drill or an arm-powered brace. Be sure you match the driver tip to the head of the screw. The wrong-sized driver will chew up the head, making it impossible to drive the screw home and equally impossible to back it out (vise grips can come to the rescue if this is the case).

33
Drive screws: Taking the time to use clamps and drill pilot holes helps guarantee an accurate, good-looking, and hassle-free job.

How to manage glue

When you really want to be sure a wooden assembly is not going to come apart, use water-resistant outdoor glue along with screws or nails. Most hardware stores carry yellow carpentry glue in an outdoor formula. Spread the glue with a small disposable paint roller. Always clamp a glued assembly before you reinforce it with screws and nails.

1 & 2
Glue it: Spread outdoor-grade yellow glue with a disposable paint roller

3
Bag it: When you're done, seal the roller and its tray inside a freezer bag. It will keep for weeks.

pieces into perfect alignment, and tighten the clamp.

- Drill a pilot hole for each screw. In softwood you can get away with a straight hole that is slightly smaller than the solid part of the screw. Or you can use a special bit made especially for drilling pilot holes, as shown in picture 31, page 25. It will simultaneously make a countersunk hole in the top piece that is just large enough for the screw to slide though, with a smaller hole in the bottom piece so the screw threads can bite in.

- Drive the screws with a muscle-powered screwdriver or with a screwdriver bit in your electric drill.

Mounting the birdhouse

Most of the birdhouses in this book are screwed to a mounting stake, which allows them to be fastened to a post or a wall. A number of stake variations are used throughout the book, notably the Bluebird house (page 39), where a pair of U-bolts connect the stake to an iron pipe.

Some birdhouses are designed to sit atop a post or pole, without a mounting stake. As shown in the diagrams, these need to be screwed to an intermediary wooden plate (picture 35), for wooden posts, or to a metal flange, for metal pipes (picture 34).

Which is better, wood posts or metal poles? The wooden post usually is more attractive, but it invites climbing predators such as cats and raccoons, and you will need to devise some sort of barrier to keep them from lunching on the eggs or nestlings. A metal pole requires some workable mounting strategy, but if it is smooth it will deter most predators.

What about nailing the birdhouse to a tree? Aside from predator access, the problem is that trees increase their girth every year. Nails or screws will either rust out or slowly disappear into the wood, crushing the birdhouse or pushing it off its moorings. Some people get around this by loosely fitting long aluminum nails in extra-large holes, so the house will slide on the nails as the tree grows. Others sidestep it by hanging the birdhouse against the tree trunk from a light chain that goes all the way around the trunk (page 73). All of these strategies have been used in the projects shown in this book.

34
To mount a birdhouse, screw it to a metal flange above a metal pipe.
35
An alternative is to screw the birdhouse to a wooden plate to sit atop a wooden post.
36
Another alternative is to screw a mounting stake to the back of the birdhouse, and then screw the stake to a pole.

Birdhouse dimensions

Each species of cavity-nesting bird has its own preferences regarding the size of the opening and of the nest box itself, as well as for house placement. The following chart gives these specifications for many common species. Remember, however, that birds don't carry tape measures, and natural cavities aren't neat and rectangular. These dimensions are guidelines, not rigid prescriptions.

	Box floor in inches	Box floor in millimeters	Box height in inches	Box height in millimeters	Entrance wid in inches
American robin	7 x 8	175 x 200	8	200	2
Barn owl	10 x 18	250 x 450	15 to 18	380 to 450	7
Barn swallow	6 x 6	150 x 150	6	150	2
Barred owl	12 x 12	300 x 300	20 to 24	500 to 600	6
Bewicks' wren	4 x 4	100 x 100	6 to 8	150 to 200	1¼
Bluebird	5 x 5	125 x 125	8 to 12	200 to 300	1⅓ to 1½

trance width millimeters	Entrance height in inches	Entrance height in millimeters	House height in feet	House height in meters	Habitat
	2	50	6 to 15	1.8 to 4.5	Backyard near buildings, often prefer open shelf
5	4	100	12 to 18	3.6 to 5.4	Large tree trunk or high hideaway
	2	50	8 to 12	2.4 to 3.6	Backyards, near buildings, near water, under bridges
0	14	355	15 to 20	4.5 to 6	
	4 to 6	100 to 150	5 to 10	1.5 to 3	
to 37	6 to 10	150 to 250	5 to 10	1.5 to 3	Open fields

	Box floor in inches	Box floor in millimeters	Box height in inches	Box height in millimeters	Entrance width in inches
Bufflehead	7 x 7	175 x 175	16	400	2⅞
Carolina wren	4 x 4	100 x 100	6 to 8	150 to 200	1½
Chickadee	4 x 4	100 x 100	9	225	1¼
Common and northern flicker	7 x 7	175 x 175	16 to 18	400 to 450	2½
Common goldeneye	12 x 12	300 x 300	24	600	4 to 5
Common merganser	9 x 9 to 11 x 11	225 x 225 to 280 x 280	33 to 40	840 to 1000	5
Downy woodpecker	4 x 4	100 x 100	8 to 10	200 to 250	1¼
Downy woodpecker	4 x 4	100 x 100	12 to 15	300 to 380	1¼
Flycatchers	6 x 6	150 x 150	8 to 12	200 to 300	1½ to 1¾

trance width millimeters	Entrance height in inches	Entrance height in millimeters	House height in feet	House height in meters	Habitat
	13 to 14	330 to 355	10 to 20	3 to 6	
	4 to 6	100 to 150	5 to 10	1.5 to 3	
	7	175	4 to 15	1.2 to 4.5	Woods edges, clearings
	14 to 16	355 to 400	6 to 20	1.8 to 6	Open fields, woods clearings
0 to 125	20 to 22	500 to 558	4 to 20	1.2 to 6	
5	28 to 35	710 to 890	8 to 20	2.4 to 6	
	6 to 8	150 to 200	5 to 15	1.5 to 4.5	Woods edges, clearings
	9 to 12	225 to 300	12 to 20	3.6 to 6	Woods edges, clearings
to 45	6 to 10	150 to 250	5 to 15	1.5 to 4.5	Open fields, desert, edge of woods

	Box floor in inches	Box floor in millimeters	Box height in inches	Box height in millimeters	Entrance width in inches
Golden-fronted woodpecker	6 x 6	150 x 150	12 to 15	300 to 380	2
Great-crested flycatcher	6 x 6	150 x 150	8 to 10	200 to 250	1½
Hairy woodpecker	6 x 6	150 x 150	12 to 15	300 to 380	1½
House finch	6 x 6	150 x 150	6	150	2
House sparrow	4 x 4 to 5 x 5	100 x 100 to 125 x 125	9 to 12	225 to 300	1⅓ to 2
Jackdaw	8 x 8	200 x 200	12	300	6
Kestrel	8 x 8	200 x 200	12 to 15	300 to 380	3
Nuthatch	4 x 4	100 x 100	9	225	1¼ to 1⅓
Phoebe	6 x 6	150 x 150	6	150	2

trance width millimeters	Entrance height in inches	Entrance height in millimeters	House height in feet	House height in meters	Habitat
	9 to 12	225 to 300	12 to 20	3.6 to 6	
	6 to 8	150 to 200	8 to 20	2.4 to 6	
	9 to 12	225 to 300	10 to 20	3 to 6	Woods edges, clearings
	4	100	8 to 12	2.4 to 3.6	Backyards, near buildings
to 50	6 to 7	150 to 175	8 to 12	2.4 to 3.6	Backyards, near buildings
	6	150	10 to 20	3 to 6	
	9 to 12	225 to 300	10 to 30	3 to 9	
to 35	7	175	5 to 15	1.5 to 4.5	Woods edges, clearings
	2	50	8 to 12	2.4 to 3.6	Backyards, near buildings, near water, under bridges; often prefer open shelves

	Box floor in inches	Box floor in millimeters	Box height in inches	Box height in millimeters	Entrance width in inches
Pileated wood-pecker	8 x 8	200 x 200	16 to 24	400 to 600	3 x 4
Prothonotary warbler	5 x 5	125 x 125	6	150	$1\frac{1}{64}$
Purple martin	6 x 6	150 x 150	6	150	$1\frac{3}{4}$ to $2\frac{1}{4}$
Red-bellied woodpecker	6 x 6	150 x 150	12 to 15	300 to 380	$2\frac{1}{2}$
Red-headed woodpecker	6 x 6	150 x 150	12 to 15	300 to 380	2
Saw-whet owl	6 x 6	150 x 150	10 to 12	250 to 300	$2\frac{1}{2}$
Screech owl	8 x 8	200 x 200	12 to 15	300 to 380	3
Titmouse	4 x 4	100 x 100	10	250	$1\frac{1}{4}$
Tree swallow	5 x 5	125 x 125	6 to 8	150 to 200	$1\frac{1}{2}$

ntrance width millimeters	Entrance height in inches	Entrance height in millimeters	House height in feet	House height in meters	Habitat
x 100	12 to 20	300 to 500	15 to 25	4.5 to 7.6	Woods edges, clearings
	4 to 5	100 to 125	4 to 8	1.2 to 2.4	Above or facing water, swamps
to 57	1 to 2	25 to 50	10 to 20	3 to 6	Open fields
	9 to 12	225 to 300	10 to 20	3 to 6	Woods edges, clearings
	9 to 12	225 to 300	12 to 20	3.6 to 6	Woods edges, clearings
	8 to 10	200 to 250	12 to 20	3.6 to 6	Open field
	9 to 12	225 to 300	10 to 30	3 to 9	Woods edges, clearings
	7	175	5 to 15	1.5 to 4.5	Woods edges, clearings; back-yard near buildings
	4 to 6	100 to 150	5 to 15	1.5 to 4.5	Open fields

	Box floor in inches	Box floor in millimeters	Box height in inches	Box height in millimeters	Entrance width in inches
Violet-green swallow	5 x 5	125 x 125	6 to 8	150 to 200	1½
Wood duck	10 x 18	250 x 450	10 to 24	250 to 600	4
Wren	4 x 4	100 x 100	6 to 8	150 to 200	1 to 1¼
Yellow-bellied sapsucker	5 x 5	125 x 125	12 to 15	300 to 380	1½

trance width millimeters	Entrance height in inches	Entrance height in millimeters	House height in feet	House height in meters	Habitat
	4 to 6	100 to 150	5 to 15	1.5 to 4.5	
o	12 to 16	300 to 400	10 to 20	3 to 6	Above or facing water, swamps
to 30	4 to 6	100 to 150	5 to 10	1.5 to 3	Woods edges, clearings; backyard near buildings
	9 to 12	225 to 300	10 to 20	3 to 6	Woods edges, clearings; large tree or high hideaway

Basic birdhouse

This basic birdhouse can be sized to meet the needs of most cavity-nesting birds. It is simple to build, so it is a good introduction to birdhouse building techniques. It also incorporates a number of fine points that make any birdhouse into a nest box that has a good chance of being occupied.

This basic birdhourse is made of untreated softwood—pine, fir, or cedar—that is ¾in (20mm) thick. This type of wood is suitable because paint, preservatives, and the glue in plywood can harm the birds.

An extended, sloping roof shades the house and keeps the rain out and a saw kerf underneath the high edge of the roof acts as a drip edge, keeping rain from running into the box. The inside surfaces are left as rough wood, to help fledglings move around and climb out.

The recessed floor has mitered corners, or else drainage holes, so water can escape. The floor locks in place, but is easy to remove for cleaning after the nesting season. Alternatively, hinge the front or one side of the box.

The front and back are set down from the roof, making ventilation slots. As an alternative, drill ½in (12mm) ventilation holes high up on both sides of the box.

There are no outside perches, because the birds that use them are nuisance starlings and house sparrows. Perches also might help other predators gain access. A double-thick plate surrounds the entrance hole, so cats and raccoons cannot reach inside.

A U-bolt and stake mounting system allows the birdhouse to be fastened atop a smooth metal pipe, which predators cannot climb. These are general points that can be adapted to most birdhouse designs, even the flamboyantly ornamental, as is seen in other projects from this book.

Predatory cats and raccoons cannot climb the smooth metal pipe supporting this orchard birdhouse. Double wood at the entry also discourages predators.

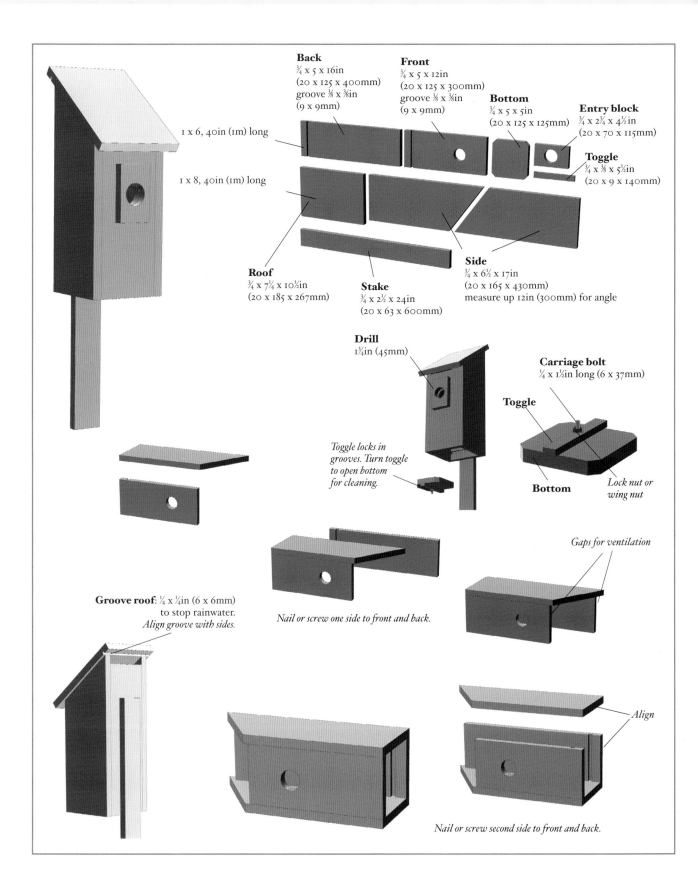

Back
¾ x 5 x 16in
(20 x 125 x 400mm)
groove ⅜ x ⅜in
(9 x 9mm)

Front
¾ x 5 x 12in
(20 x 125 x 300mm)
groove ⅜ x ⅜in
(9 x 9mm)

Bottom
¾ x 5 x 5in
(20 x 125 x 125mm)

Entry block
¾ x 2¾ x 4½in
(20 x 70 x 115mm)

Toggle
¾ x ⅜ x 5½in
(20 x 9 x 140mm)

1 x 6, 40in (1m) long

1 x 8, 40in (1m) long

Roof
¾ x 7¼ x 10½in
(20 x 185 x 267mm)

Stake
¾ x 2½ x 24in
(20 x 63 x 600mm)

Side
¾ x 6½ x 17in
(20 x 165 x 430mm)
measure up 12in (300mm) for angle

Drill
1¾in (45mm)

Carriage bolt
¼ x 1½in long (6 x 37mm)

Toggle

Bottom

Lock nut or wing nut

Toggle locks in grooves. Turn toggle to open bottom for cleaning.

Groove roof: ¼ x ¼in (6 x 6mm) to stop rainwater. *Align groove with sides.*

Nail or screw one side to front and back.

Gaps for ventilation

Align

Nail or screw second side to front and back.

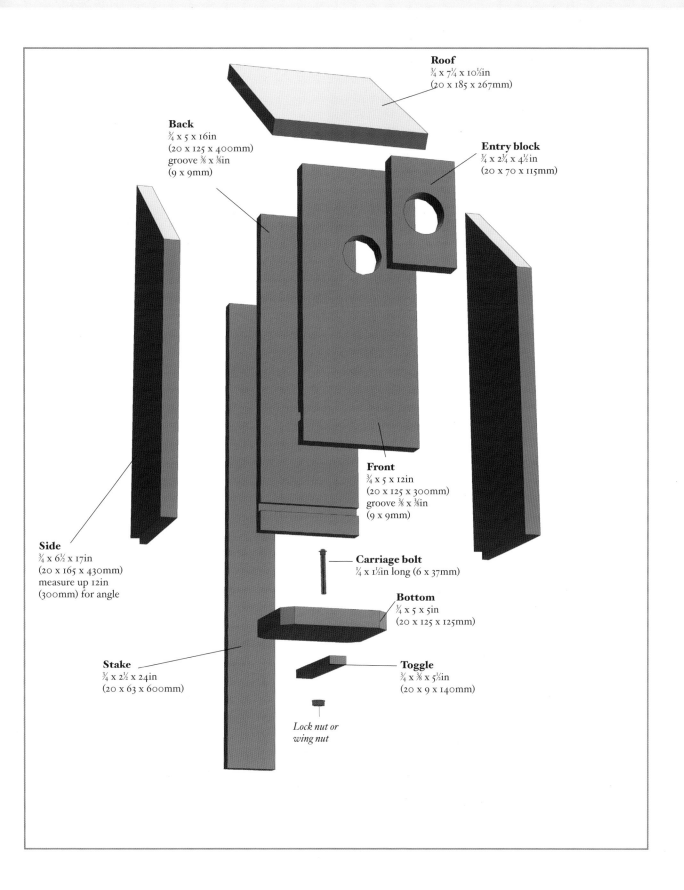

Roof
¾ x 7¼ x 10½in
(20 x 185 x 267mm)

Back
¾ x 5 x 16in
(20 x 125 x 400mm)
groove ⅜ x ⅜in
(9 x 9mm)

Entry block
¾ x 2¾ x 4½in
(20 x 70 x 115mm)

Side
¾ x 6½ x 17in
(20 x 165 x 430mm)
measure up 12in
(300mm) for angle

Front
¾ x 5 x 12in
(20 x 125 x 300mm)
groove ⅜ x ⅜in
(9 x 9mm)

Carriage bolt
¼ x 1½in long (6 x 37mm)

Bottom
¾ x 5 x 5in
(20 x 125 x 125mm)

Stake
¾ x 2½ x 24in
(20 x 63 x 600mm)

Toggle
¾ x ⅜ x 5½in
(20 x 9 x 140mm)

*Lock nut or
wing nut*

41

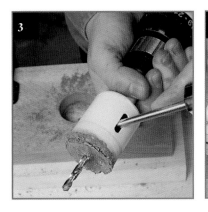

1

Cut all the parts. Use a lock nut a wing nut to fasten the toggle (see Making a Toggle) to the birdhouse floor. Note that the corners have been sawn off the floor, to make drainage openings.

2

Use a hole saw to cut the bird entry. The hole saw used here makes a 1¾in (45mm) hole, suitable for Eastern bluebirds. (Consult the charts in the Birdhouse Woodworking section for other species, and for the height of the entry hole.)

3

Insert a large screwdriver into the hole saw slots and pry the plug off the centering bit. Save the hole saw plugs as they make good wheels for toy cars and trucks.

4

Lay the first side flat on the workbench to start the nails. Use three nails along each edge. Drive one of them so it just comes through the other side of the wood. The sides have been grooved so they will retain the bottom, following the procedure in step 8 (see also Making a Toggle steps 1 & 2).

5

Set the side in place on the birdhouse front and press it in place so the single protruding nail starts into the front. Drive all three nails. Here the back has been positioned to support the side for nailing; fasten it in place next.

6

Turn the assembly over and position the second side. Draw a layout line to help you position the nails; for best results, start them with the wood flat on the bench as you did with the first side.

7

Nail the second side to the front and back of the birdhouse. The clamp used here is pulling the sides together a smidgen; do what you can to keep the house square and neat.

8 & 9

Before attaching the roof, make a drip groove near the back edge. The groove will keep rainwater from running down inside the house. Saw both sides of the groove about ¼in (6mm) deep. Then push a narrow chisel into the groove to remove the waste wood. There are many ways to make a groove like this (see Birdhouse Woodworking section).

10

Nail the roof onto the sides. Position the roof so the lower edge of the drip groove lines up with the top corners of the sides. The ventilation gap front and rear is essential.

11

Insert the removeable bottom and turn the toggle into the grooves to lock it in place. The fit should be comfortably snug but not tight.

12

Use two U-bolts to fasten the birdhouse onto a metal pole. Drill the stake for the U-bolts, insert them and start the nuts.

13 & 14

Screw the mounting stake to the back of the birdhouse. Use three screws placed in a triangular pattern.

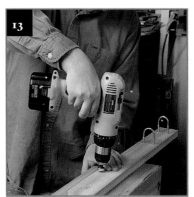 

15 & 16

Drill an entry-sized hole in the wood that will become the entry block. Drill the hole in a long piece of wood that you can clamp to the workbench, then saw the block off the wood.

17

Nail the entry block to the front of the birdhouse. This double thickness of wood prevents raccoons and cats from reaching inside to snag eggs and hatchlings.

Making a toggle

Birdhouses need to be cleaned out soon after each clutch of fledglings sets forth in the world, which means you need to be able to open the house. One common solution is a hinge and a latch, as seen on a number of the birdhouses in this book. It works, but never perfectly and it is always jarring to see. Another common solution is a removable side held in place by one or two screws, also used by several of the houses in this book. This also works and does not look bad, but in the field you need to have remembered to pocket a screwdriver, and a well-situated birdhouse probably is not all that easy to get at for removing the screws. A good solution to all these problems is the toggle bottom. A pivoting toggle is bolted to the birdhouse floor. It turns into and out of a groove cut in the box sides. This following sequence shows a simple way to make it.

1, 2, & 3

To make the groove, draw a pair of parallel lines across the birdhouse side, about 1in (25mm) up from the end and ¼in (6mm) apart. Saw both lines down to about halfway through the wood. Break the waste wood out of the groove with a wide chisel.

4 & 5

To make the toggle, saw a strip of wood to a little thicker than the width of the groove. Check how it fits and whittle it or sand the end of the stick to an easy fit. Then place the toggle across the birdhouse floor to mark the length, which should be just long enough to bottom in the groove.

6

Drill a ¼in (6mm) hole through the center of the toggle, and the center of the birdhouse floor. Connect the two pieces with a 1½in (37mm) carriage bolt. Start the bolt through the floor first. Secure it with a flat washer and a wing nut or a locking nut.

7 & 8

With the birdhouse box assembled, make sure the floor fits easily into the opening. Turn the toggle into the groove. If it bottoms, turn it tight against the wood so it jams in place.

Roof birdhouse

Here is a basic birdhouse with a peaked roof, so it looks like a house instead of a chicken coop. It can be sized to suit most species of bird, it can be detailed to meet the bird-friendly criteria detailed on the basic birdhouse, and it can be painted to suit your garden décor.

Peaked-roof boxes like this are the basic building unit for more complex birdhouses. These bird boxes can be stacked (see the big birdhouse project, page 76), or joined side to side for birds such as wrens that will nest near one another.

The roof of the house shown here was made from shakes, which makes them look hobbity or elvish. If you make the roof with a steeper pitch, the house will start to look like a church; if you make the pitch shallower, it will look more like a cottage or hut.

This project shows how to bevel the sides for a neat and tight fit against the roof. However, doing it this way requires drilling some ventilation holes under the eaves, lest the hatchlings cook under the July sun. The alternative is to leave the sides square and set them down ¼in (6mm) to ⅜in (9mm) from the roof, for easy ventilation.

The roof of this house is removable for cleaning. It is held in place by two brass screws, one through each gable into the ridge block. As an alternative, you could nail the roof to the back and sides, and hinge the front to the floor, or you could make a toggle floor, as shown in the basic birdhouse project.

The roof of this simple birdhouse is made from split cedar barn shakes. The roof can be removed for spring cleaning.

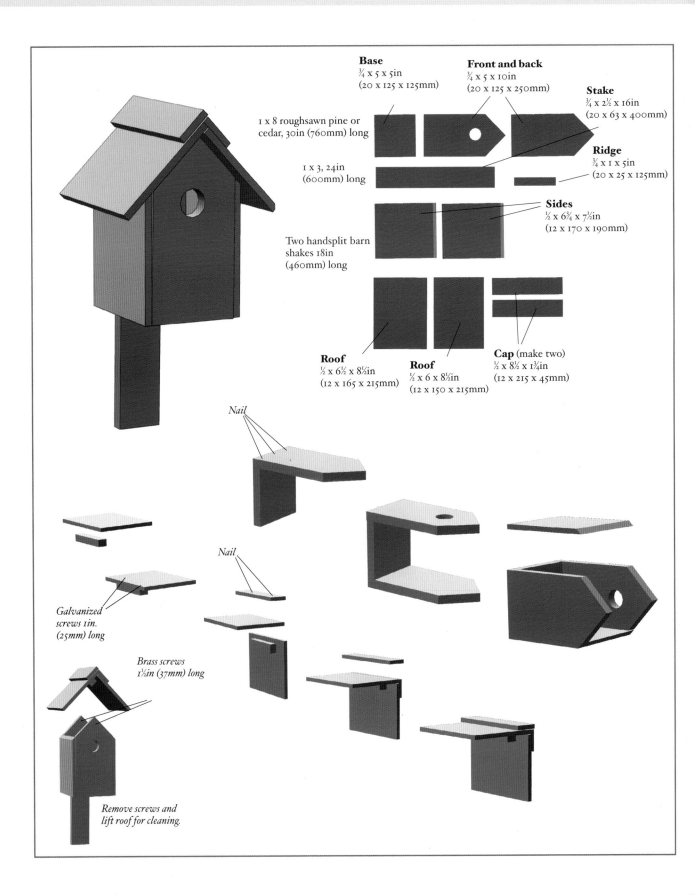

Base
¾ x 5 x 5in
(20 x 125 x 125mm)

Front and back
¾ x 5 x 10in
(20 x 125 x 250mm)

Stake
¾ x 2½ x 16in
(20 x 63 x 400mm)

1 x 8 roughsawn pine or
cedar, 30in (760mm) long

Ridge
¾ x 1 x 5in
(20 x 25 x 125mm)

1 x 3, 24in
(600mm) long

Sides
½ x 6¾ x 7½in
(12 x 170 x 190mm)

Two handsplit barn
shakes 18in
(460mm) long

Roof
½ x 6½ x 8½in
(12 x 165 x 215mm)

Roof
½ x 6 x 8½in
(12 x 150 x 215mm)

Cap (make two)
½ x 8½ x 1¾in
(12 x 215 x 45mm)

Nail

Nail

*Galvanized
screws 1in.
(25mm) long*

*Brass screws
1½in (37mm) long*

*Remove screws and
lift roof for cleaning.*

48

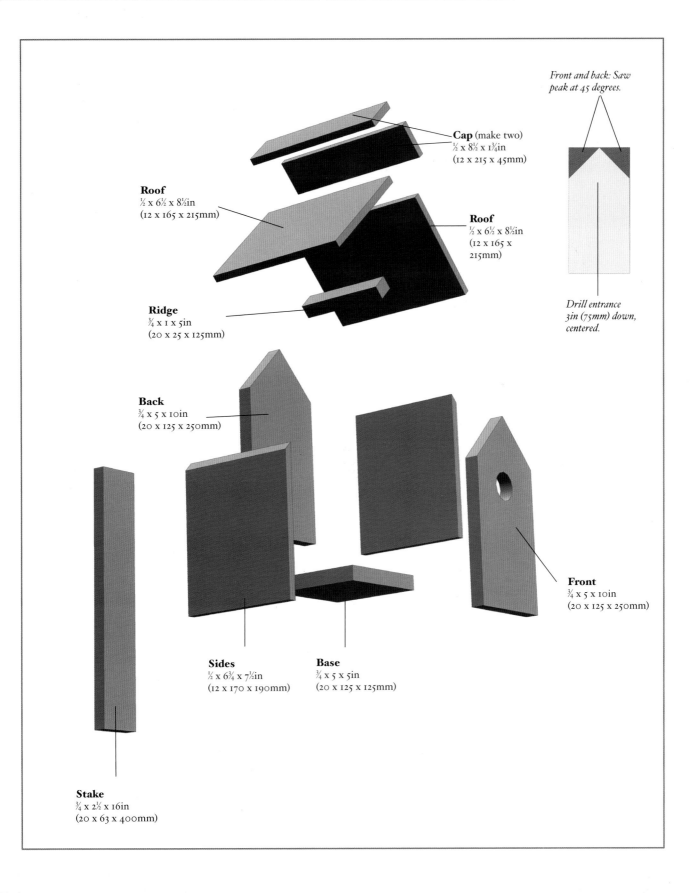

Front and back: Saw peak at 45 degrees.

Cap (make two)
½ x 8½ x 1¾in
(12 x 215 x 45mm)

Roof
½ x 6½ x 8½in
(12 x 165 x 215mm)

Roof
½ x 6½ x 8½in
(12 x 165 x 215mm)

Ridge
¾ x 1 x 5in
(20 x 25 x 125mm)

Drill entrance 3in (75mm) down, centered.

Back
¾ x 5 x 10in
(20 x 125 x 250mm)

Front
¾ x 5 x 10in
(20 x 125 x 250mm)

Sides
½ x 6¾ x 7½in
(12 x 170 x 190mm)

Base
¾ x 5 x 5in
(20 x 125 x 125mm)

Stake
¾ x 2½ x 16in
(20 x 63 x 400mm)

49

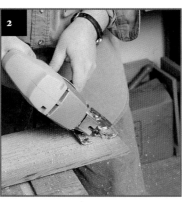

1

Set the jigsaw angle to 45 degrees (the angle for the birdhouse sides and gables) and tighten it securely.

2

Saw the beveled sides: Clamp the wood for the sides to the workbench so it overhangs one end, make a layout line, and steer the saw straight through the wood.

3

Find the size of the entry hole preferred by the birds you wish to attract (see Birdhouse Woodworking section). Measure the location of the entry hole, and drill it. An adjustable auger bit was used here, a very handy tool to have.

4

Unlike the basic birdhouse project, this birdhouse has a base that is not removeable. Drive three galvanized siding nails through the front and the back. Be sure to drill some drainage holes in the bottom too.

5 & 6

Use the square to position the sides of the birdhouse and make a continuous bevel from the top edge of the sides to the roof gables. Nail the sides to the ends and bottom, using galvanized siding nails.

7 & 8

Hold the two main roof pieces in place and position the ridge, to which both sides of the roof will be fastened. Draw a layout line around the ridge block on one of the roof pieces. Clamp the ridge block on the layout lines.

9 & 10

Turn the subassembly over so you can drill pilot holes through the roof into the ridge block. Then screw the two pieces securely together. Use two 1in (25mm) galvanized screws.

11

Once you have attached the ridge block to one of the roof pieces, it is easy to position the other roof piece and screw it in place in the same way.

12

When you use rough-split shakes, there will always be some gaps in the roof. That is why you add a cap, that is, two strips sawn from a cedar shake. Nail the cap through the roof into the ridge block.

13

Finally, drill pilot holes and drive a brass screw through the gable front and back, into the ridge block. These two screws can be removed, so you can lift the roof and clean out the birdhouse. Center the mounting stake on the back of the birdhouse and fasten it there with screws or nails. Fasten it to a metal or wooden post.

Bluebird house

Bluebirds seem to prefer a house that does not have a wide, flat floor—perhaps a shape like this seems more like a tree cavity. People like this style of house too, because it looks cozy and cute. It is also a good style to paint, but be sure to keep the paint on the outside only, and just come up to the edge of the opening.

This house has a hinged side, that drops open to allow inspection and cleaning. A wire twist-tie through a pair of screw eyes ensures the house is closed to predators—remember that raccoons can open a regular hook-and-eye. The twist-tie is beyond a raccoon's ability, but easy for you to open so you can inspect the nestlings.

Don't worry about handling the house while the nestlings are inside. Experienced birders say the idea that human scent will drive the parent birds away is false, an old-wives tale. So far as we know, birds don't have much of a sense of smell. If you should open the house and a nestling falls out, gently pick it up and put it back.

Camouflage paint fades this traditional bluebird house into the evergreen mountain laurel. Prime the house, paint it dark brown all over, then streak and splotch with sunny, leafy green. Finally, stencil a few strong leaves on the roof and front.

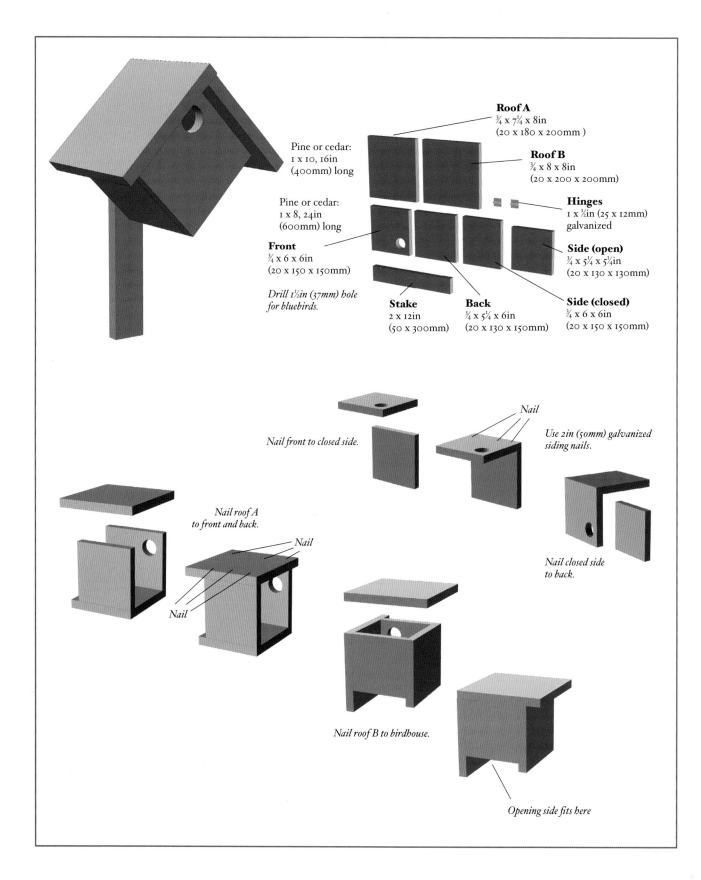

Pine or cedar:
1 x 10, 16in
(400mm) long

Pine or cedar:
1 x 8, 24in
(600mm) long

Roof A
¾ x 7¼ x 8in
(20 x 180 x 200mm)

Roof B
¾ x 8 x 8in
(20 x 200 x 200mm)

Hinges
1 x ½in (25 x 12mm)
galvanized

Front
¾ x 6 x 6in
(20 x 150 x 150mm)

Drill 1½in (37mm) hole
for bluebirds.

Side (open)
¾ x 5¼ x 5¼in
(20 x 130 x 130mm)

Stake
2 x 12in
(50 x 300mm)

Back
¾ x 5¼ x 6in
(20 x 130 x 150mm)

Side (closed)
¾ x 6 x 6in
(20 x 150 x 150mm)

Nail front to closed side.

Nail

Use 2in (50mm) galvanized
siding nails.

*Nail roof A
to front and back.*

Nail

Nail

Nail closed side
to back.

Nail roof B to birdhouse.

Opening side fits here

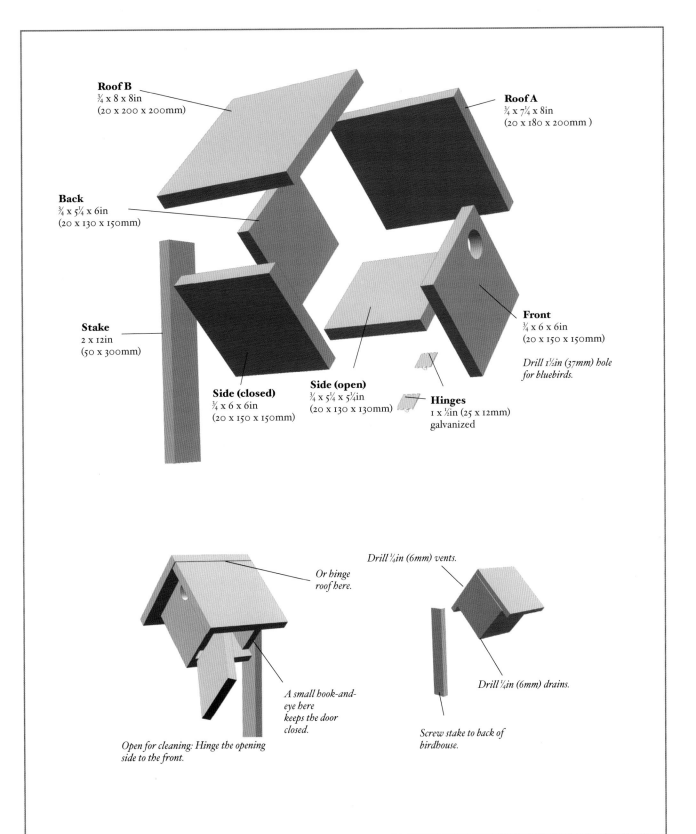

Roof B
¾ x 8 x 8in
(20 x 200 x 200mm)

Roof A
¾ x 7¼ x 8in
(20 x 180 x 200mm)

Back
¾ x 5¼ x 6in
(20 x 130 x 150mm)

Stake
2 x 12in
(50 x 300mm)

Side (closed)
¾ x 6 x 6in
(20 x 150 x 150mm)

Side (open)
¾ x 5¼ x 5¼in
(20 x 130 x 130mm)

Front
¾ x 6 x 6in
(20 x 150 x 150mm)

*Drill 1½in (37mm) hole
for bluebirds.*

Hinges
1 x ½in (25 x 12mm)
galvanized

*Or hinge
roof here.*

*A small hook-and-
eye here
keeps the door
closed.*

*Open for cleaning: Hinge the opening
side to the front.*

Drill ¼in (6mm) vents.

Drill ¼in (6mm) drains.

*Screw stake to back of
birdhouse.*

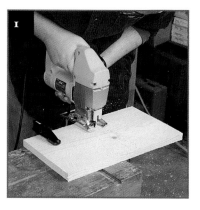

1

Draw a square line at the length you want and steer the jigsaw across the pine. Clamp the wood so it overhangs the end of the workbench. For safety reasons, never try to hand-hold it for sawing.

2 & 3

Saw the parts that are 8in (200mm) wide from 1 x 10 pine boards. Measure the width and draw a layout line, and clamp the wood so it overhangs the workbench. Saw as close as you can to the outside of the line.

4

A small Surform file, the throw-away equivalent of a block plane, removes any sawing irregularities from the new edge.

5 & 6

Whether you are using an electric drill or this old-style brace-and-bit, always clamp the birdhouse front to the workbench, atop a protective board. When it is sharp, the adjustable auger cuts a nice shaving. Sharpen it with a small, fine file.

7

Nail or screw the front of the birdhouse to the closed side piece, then nail through the side piece into the back. Fit the opening side piece into place and mark the hinge edge.

8 & 9

Place the hinges on the wood so you can draw around them, and locate the screws with pencil marks. Make pilot holes for the hinge screws using an awl or small drill bit.

10 & 11

Turn the screws into their pilot holes. The screws are small, but so is the wood, and if you skip drilling the holes, it probably will split.

12

Screw the other leaf of the hinges to the birdhouse in the same way. Having the hinged door in place makes it much easier to attach the two pieces of the roof.

13
Fit the smaller of the two roof pieces (Roof A) onto the body of the birdhouse. The other roof piece (Roof B) overlaps the edge of this one. Square layout lines for the nails across the roof pieces.

14
Start three nails into the wood along the layout lines.

15
Hold the roof piece in position on the walls while you drive the nails home.

16
Drill three ¼in (6 mm) holes near the peak of the back wall, for ventilation. Drill three more into the bottom of the house, so water can drain.

17 & 18

Center the mounting stake on the back of the birdhouse. Fasten it there with three or four 1¼in (30mm)
screws using a drill.

19

Keep the birdhouse closed with a tight hook-and-eye, or
a pair of screw eyes locked together with a wire twist-tie.
Use the awl to make a pilot hole and also to help twist
the eye into the wood.

20

Dub the sharp corners off the wood by sanding with
100-grit paper on a hard block. This cosmetic step is
especially important if you plan to paint the birdhouse,
since paint does not stick to a sharp corner.

21

The back view of the completed birdhouse shows the
door hook, ventilation holes, and mounting stake. Use a
pair of U-bolts to attach the stake to a smooth metal
pipe that predators can't climb.

Cube house

The cube house hangs from its top corner. Drill a hole through the top corner to install an eye-bolt with nuts and washers, and suspend it on a light chain. Don't use a screw eye, nor a rope or string. You've got to be sure the house won't come crashing down due to the weather (sunlight degrades many kinds of rope and string) or from the desire of other small animals to unravel rope and steal it for their own nesting materials.

The birdhouse opens into two parts when you remove three brass screws. As an alternative, you can hinge the two parts. However, if you do that, hold the house closed by linking two small screw eyes with a wire twist-tie, as shown on the bluebird house project.

If you like the spare geometry of this birdhouse, try varying the size of the three roof pieces. You can make them wider and longer, and from different materials like shingles and barn shakes.

This style of house is suitable for painting, on the outside and only up to the entry protector. We make them with a white roof and a colored body, and with roof and body in two shades of the same color.

The simple geometry of the cube house cries out for simple and solid colors. You cannot go wrong by choosing two closely related hues.

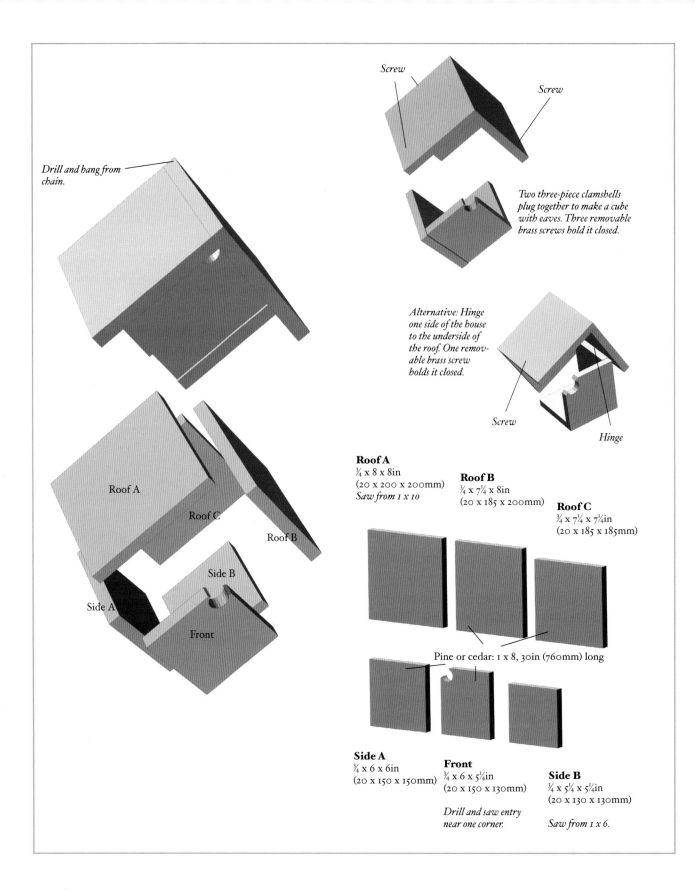

Drill and hang from chain.

Screw

Screw

Two three-piece clamshells plug together to make a cube with eaves. Three removable brass screws hold it closed.

Alternative: Hinge one side of the house to the underside of the roof. One removable brass screw holds it closed.

Screw

Hinge

Roof A
Roof C
Roof B

Side B
Side A
Front

Roof A
¾ x 8 x 8in
(20 x 200 x 200mm)
Saw from 1 x 10

Roof B
¾ x 7¼ x 8in
(20 x 185 x 200mm)

Roof C
¾ x 7¼ x 7¼in
(20 x 185 x 185mm)

Pine or cedar: 1 x 8, 30in (760mm) long

Side A
¾ x 6 x 6in
(20 x 150 x 150mm)

Front
¾ x 6 x 5¼in
(20 x 150 x 130mm)

Drill and saw entry near one corner.

Side B
¾ x 5¼ x 5¼in
(20 x 130 x 130mm)

Saw from 1 x 6.

1 & 2

The cube house has two similar halves that fit together like woody clamshells. Each half is made of three pieces that are almost the same size, starting with a square and trimming the wood's thickness off one way and then both ways.

3

Drill the front piece near one corner, leaving a little web of wood between the hole and the nearby edges. (The front piece is the middle–sized rectangular one in the smaller set of three pieces.)

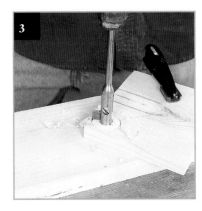

4

Saw across the little web of wood. This Japanese-style dozuki saw cuts on the pull stroke. A little Xacto saw, or a regular dovetail or tenon saw, will also make a neat cut

5

Fit three pieces together (as in 2) and mark which edges mate. With the wood flat on the bench, start two or three galvanized siding nails along the first mating edge.

6

Use the third piece of wood as a prop while you drive the nails into the first joint.

7

Keeping three pieces of wood lined up can be tricky, but two 12in (30mm) clamps will take all the wobbliness out of it. With the clamps fitting just snug, use your hammer to lightly tap each piece into position. Then tighten the clamps.

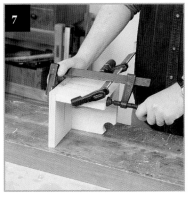

8
The two clamps act as your third hand, to help you to nail the third piece to the other two.

9, 10, & 11
Three brass screws hold the two halves of this birdhouse together. They can be turned loose in the field when it is time to clean the house. It can be tricky to see where the screws should go, so take the guesswork out of it by tracing around the house on the inside, then extend the lines over the edge to the outside.

12 & 13

The brass screws should slip easily through the first piece of wood, so they can bite cleanly into the second. Drill clearance holes the size of the screw shank, or a hair larger (see Birdhouse Woodworking section).

14

The birds need air and drainage as there cannot be water in the base of the birdhouse. Drill ⅜in (9mm) vent and drain holes near each corner of the smaller half-cube.

15

Set a hanging ring at the peak of the birdhouse roof. Use an eye-bolt with nuts and washers, not a screw eye, which can pull loose. Hang the birdhouse from a light metal chain.

Robin shelf

Robins and starlings will occupy nest boxes, but they seem to prefer an open shelf high up on the wall of a building. You will often find their nests high in the eaves of old farm buildings, or on top of the exposed roof beams of a contemporary house.

You can make robin shelves in different shapes depending on your preference. The robins probably don't care, but who knows? They are made in exactly the same way. The difference is in the curve of the side wall—one is angular, the other is S-shaped. Even though the shelf is open, if you want to encourage the birds to return then it is best to climb up there and clean it after each nesting season.

Open shelves tucked high in the eaves offer a welcome haven to robins, phoebes, and swallows.

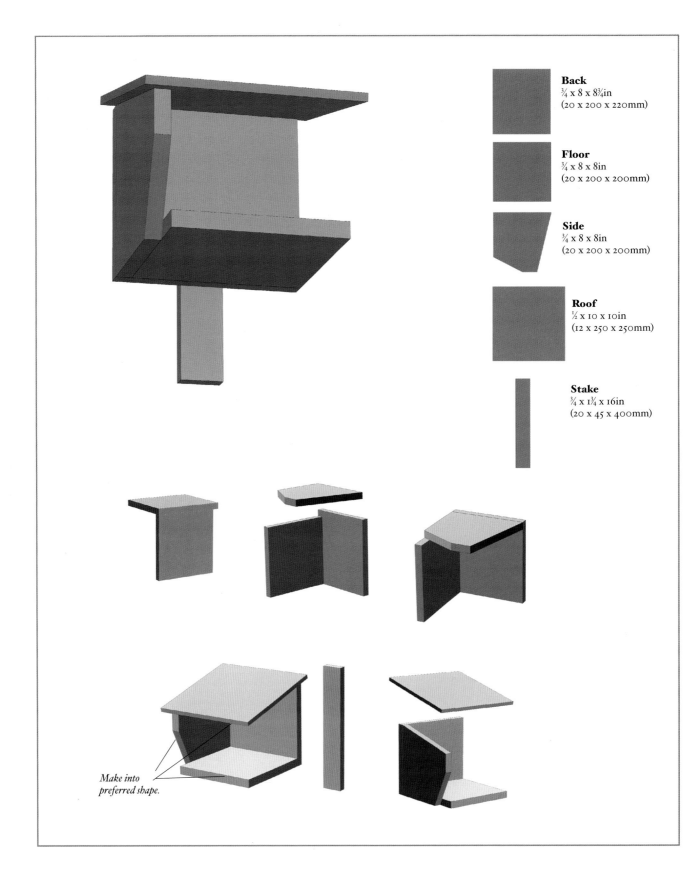

Back
¾ x 8 x 8¾in
(20 x 200 x 220mm)

Floor
¾ x 8 x 8in
(20 x 200 x 200mm)

Side
¾ x 8 x 8in
(20 x 200 x 200mm)

Roof
½ x 10 x 10in
(12 x 250 x 250mm)

Stake
¾ x 1¾ x 16in
(20 x 45 x 400mm)

*Make into
preferred shape.*

1

Cut the parts. Nail the side to the birdhouse back, then fit and nail this subassembly to the bottom piece. In effect, you are making a half-cube or wooden clamshell, the same as the cube house project.

2 & 3

Choose a wide barn shake. This material is about ½in (12mm) thick, with a rough surface because it has been split out of a cedar block. Fit the shake on the shelf and mark where you want to cut it. Then use the square to extend the mark across the wood.

4 & 5

Clamp the shake onto a bench hook and saw the layout line. The Japanese dozuki saw at left (4) cuts on the pull stroke, while the short toolbox saw at right (5) cuts on the push stroke—choose the style of saw that is most comfortable for you.

6
Use galvanized shingle nails, which are about 1¼in (30mm) long, to fasten the roof to the sides and back of the robin shelf.

7 & 8
Screw the mounting stake onto the back of the birdhouse. Use short galvanized screws so they don't come through into the living space.

9 & 10
You can make the side of the shelf any shape you like. Sketch a flowing S-shaped curve freehand, then smooth it out by tracing around a suitable can or dessert plate.

II

Steer the jigsaw along the curved line. Concentrate on keeping the saw base flat on the wood, and steer by moving forward while pivoting around the front edge of the blade. If it goes off, don't try to compensate by shoving the saw sideways. Steer toward the line while continuing to move the saw forward.

I2

The wood is soft so it is easy to correct a lumpy curve by sanding with 100-grit sandpaper, wrapped around a hard block.

I3

The completed robin shelf can be attached to a suitable metal or wooden pole.

Cat proof bird box

The extended front of this nest box is almost impossible for a cat to climb over. It is a traditional "boy scout design," the type of fodder used to gain merit badges. With a double thickness of wood at the opening, a locking catch as shown here, and the box mounted on a smooth metal pole, this little fortress is all but impregnable to any predators.

This design is very adaptable and can be made out of plywood or T-111 siding for larger critters, such as owls, wood ducks, mergansers, raccoons, and squirrels. Squirrels probably would prefer their 3in (75mm) entry hole to be someplace on the side of the box. Wood ducks prefer an oval-shaped entry measuring about 3in (75mm) wide by 4in (100mm) high. Raccoons and common mergansers need a 5in (125mm) wide by 6in (150mm) high oval-shaped opening.

A loop of light chain anchored by a couple of hooks is the best way to tree-mount a birdhouse. It is easy to remove and replace, and it does not harm the tree.

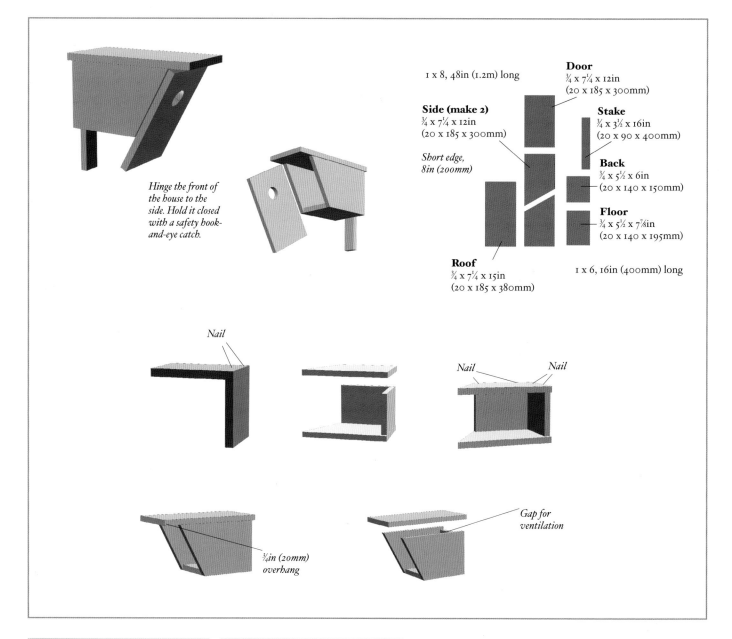

Hinge the front of the house to the side. Hold it closed with a safety hook-and-eye catch.

1 x 8, 48in (1.2m) long

Door
¾ x 7¼ x 12in
(20 x 185 x 300mm)

Side (make 2)
¾ x 7¼ x 12in
(20 x 185 x 300mm)

Short edge,
8in (200mm)

Stake
¾ x 3½ x 16in
(20 x 90 x 400mm)

Back
¾ x 5½ x 6in
(20 x 140 x 150mm)

Floor
¾ x 5½ x 7⅞in
(20 x 140 x 195mm)

Roof
¾ x 7¼ x 15in
(20 x 185 x 380mm)

1 x 6, 16in (400mm) long

Nail

Nail   Nail

¾in (20mm) overhang

Gap for ventilation

1

Cut all the parts. Nail the body of the box together following the sequence shown in the drawing above. Use galvanized siding nails and when possible, start the nails with the wood flat on the workbench.

2

Hinging the front to the roof does not work because of the angle of the front. A pair of hinges work fine when they connect the long edge of the front to the side of the birdhouse. Hold each hinge in place and mark where the screws will go with an awl.

3

Screw the hinges to the side of the birdhouse. Use small galvanized hinges with galvanized screws, else the metal will rust and freeze shut.

4

Set the birdhouse on its side so you can see where the front has to fit. Try it open as well as closed, then mark the screw locations with the point of the awl and screw the hinges to the front of the birdhouse. If it is too tight for the electric drill, use a small Phillips (cross-point) screwdriver.

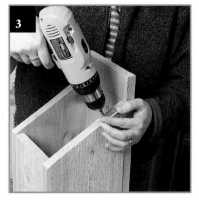

5

A guarded screw eye will lock this door. Raccoons can open an ordinary, unguarded eye. Use the awl to make a starter hole so you can twist the hook-side screw eye into the door of the birdhouse.

6

With the hook portion of the catch screwed into the door, you will be able to see and mark where the screw eye has to go.

7 & 8

Use the awl to make a starter hole, and also to get a grip on the little eye so you can twist it into the wood. The result should be tight and neat, easy enough for you to open but impossible for predators.

9

Screw the mounting stake onto the back of the birdhouse. It fits up under the rear overhang that was made when you nailed the roof onto the sides.

10

Now attach the mounting stake to a tree, a pole, or the wall of an outbuilding.

Big house

The big house looks complicated to build, but it is not. It is just a stack of basic roof-style birdhouses. Wrens and sparrows will nest in a cluster of houses like this, as will purple martins.

Stacking the houses so they face in alternate directions allows each floor to extend beyond the walls of the house below. Drill some drainage holes in the overhangs, so the houses can drain without flooding the downstairs neighbors.

Be sure you plan carefully how you will open the big house for cleaning. Here the sides of two of the houses are nailed into a single unit that is held in place with two brass screws. As an alternative, it could be hinged. These two houses sit across the bottom house, held by a brass screw through the front and back just below the roof peak. It too could be hinged instead.

The cupola is just for looks. It is a chunk of 4 x 4 post cut to a peak and roofed, with a false entry. That is, a hole drilled all the way through.

You could make this apartment birdhouse as tall as you like just by adding more boxes and false eaves. The cupola is a solid block of wood notched to fit over the roof.

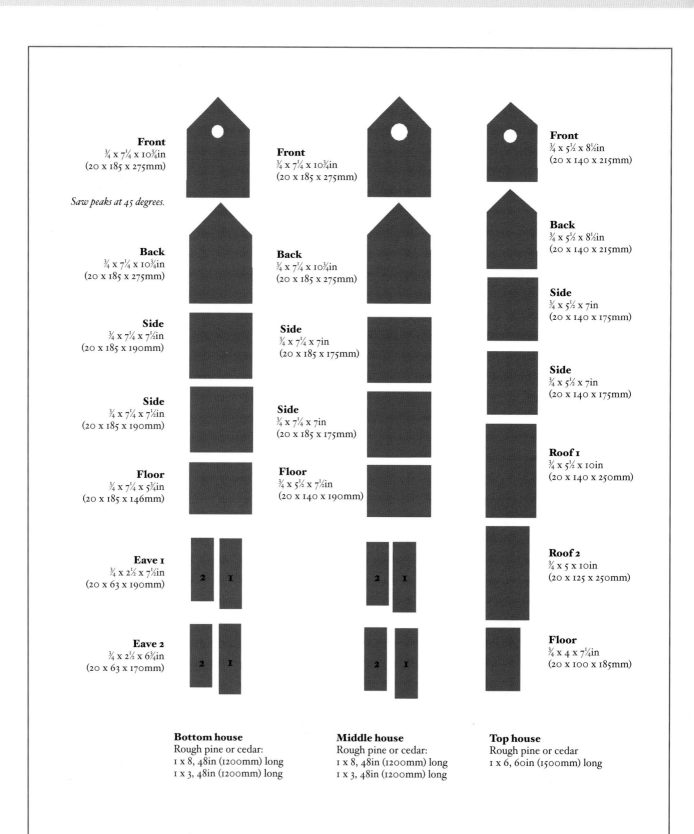

Front
¾ x 7¼ x 10¾in
(20 x 185 x 275mm)

Saw peaks at 45 degrees.

Back
¾ x 7¼ x 10¾in
(20 x 185 x 275mm)

Side
¾ x 7¼ x 7½in
(20 x 185 x 190mm)

Side
¾ x 7¼ x 7½in
(20 x 185 x 190mm)

Floor
¾ x 7¼ x 5¾in
(20 x 185 x 146mm)

Eave 1
¾ x 2½ x 7½in
(20 x 63 x 190mm)

Eave 2
¾ x 2½ x 6¾in
(20 x 63 x 170mm)

Front
¾ x 7¼ x 10¾in
(20 x 185 x 275mm)

Back
¾ x 7¼ x 10¾in
(20 x 185 x 275mm)

Side
¾ x 7¼ x 7in
(20 x 185 x 175mm)

Side
¾ x 7¼ x 7in
(20 x 185 x 175mm)

Floor
¾ x 5½ x 7½in
(20 x 140 x 190mm)

Front
¾ x 5½ x 8½in
(20 x 140 x 215mm)

Back
¾ x 5½ x 8½in
(20 x 140 x 215mm)

Side
¾ x 5½ x 7in
(20 x 140 x 175mm)

Side
¾ x 5½ x 7in
(20 x 140 x 175mm)

Roof 1
¾ x 5½ x 10in
(20 x 140 x 250mm)

Roof 2
¾ x 5 x 10in
(20 x 125 x 250mm)

Floor
¾ x 4 x 7¼in
(20 x 100 x 185mm)

Bottom house
Rough pine or cedar:
1 x 8, 48in (1200mm) long
1 x 3, 48in (1200mm) long

Middle house
Rough pine or cedar:
1 x 8, 48in (1200mm) long
1 x 3, 48in (1200mm) long

Top house
Rough pine or cedar
1 x 6, 60in (1500mm) long

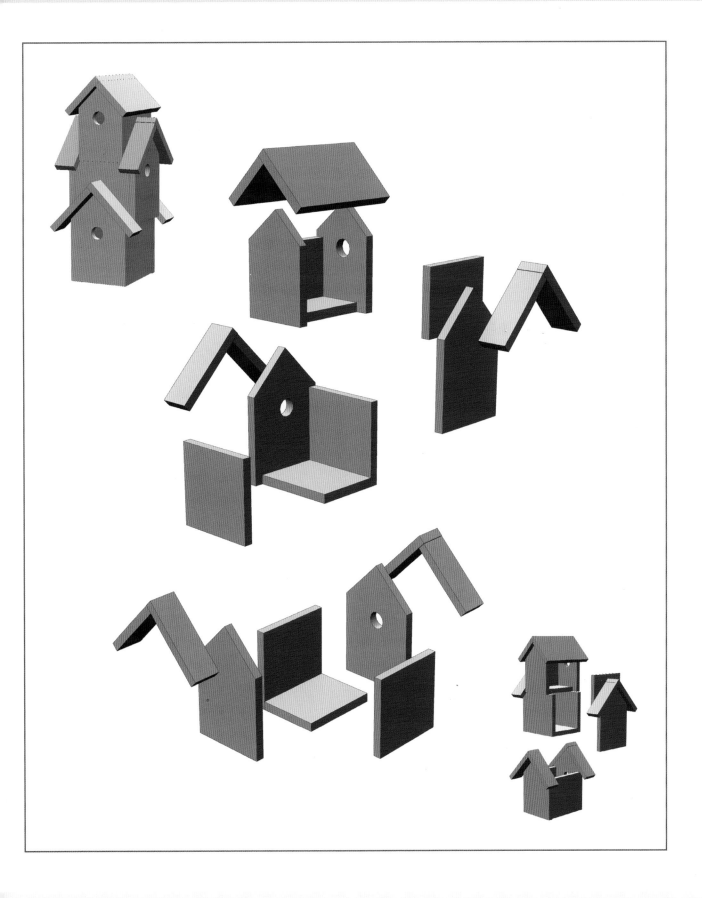

1

Saw the parts and tack them together with 12in (300mm) clamps, and see how the assembled birdhouse looks to you. You might decide to make one of the houses bigger or smaller.

2

It is usually easiest to drill the bird entry before you assemble the birdhouse. Whether you are using an electric drill or a brace-and-bit, always clamp the wood to the bench for drilling.

3, 4, & 5

Join each birdhouse together with 2in (50mm) galvanized siding nails. Draw layout lines so you can start the nails with the wood flat on the bench. Be sure you don't nail the side of one house and the back of the other—the two sides that will open for cleaning.

6

Put the top birdhouse across the second one, and nail them together. Use a stick of wood (right) to help center them and line them up.

7 & 8

The roof pitch is 45 degrees, so the angle at the peak is 90 degrees. This is so you can nail the two eaves pieces together without cutting any odd angles.

9

Nail the false roof or eaves to the front of the bottom birdhouse. Fit the eaves pieces tight against the wall of the upper house.

10

As you can see in the drawing on page 79, the eaves or false roof connects the opening side of each house. Begin by nailing the eaves to the lower peak, then hold all the pieces in place and mark where the eaves fit against the upper wall.

11 & 12

Tack the parts together with a clamp. Then place the door subassembly flat on the bench so you can nail all the pieces together.

13 & 14

Nail the two pieces of the upper roof together. Then nail the upper roof onto the birdhouse.

15 & 16

The whole side of the birdhouse comes off for fall cleaning. It is held in place by two brass screws, with clearance holes predrilled through the door so the threads can dig into the adjacent sides.

17 & 18

The third birdhouse goes together just the same as the other two. When you put all three houses together you will see where the eaves fit.

19

Saw the cupola from a scrap of square post, fit a roof on it, and nail it atop the birdhouse. We stopped at four, but you could keep going with bigger and smaller houses in both directions.

20 & 21

The two parts of the birdhouse separate for cleaning after the nesting season. The house locks closed with removable brass screws through the ridge at both ends. Be sure to drill 5/16in (8mm) drainage holes in the over-hanging floor of all three compartments. When complete attach the birdhouse to a suitable post.

Peterson bluebird house

Bluebird houses are a favorite because the birds are so beautiful. In many parts of the country, loss of woodland habitat has stressed the bluebird population. Many state wildlife services now recommend the Peterson style of house for bluebirds. It tapers inside to a small floor, so it more closely resembles a natural cavity in a tree trunk. It has an oval-shaped entry that is also more like a natural opening.

There are two different ways to build the Peterson bluebird house. Both versions have the same quadrilateral sides, which you can lay out for cutting with a jigsaw strictly by measuring distances, as shown on the drawing on the following pages. If you're using a chop saw or a table saw, the miter angle is 27 degrees.

The body of one version is sawn from about 5ft (1.5m) of 1 x 4 material using a handsaw or jigsaw. All the cuts are square crosscuts, there are no end-miters. This version of the house can be held together with galvanized screws or siding nails.

The other version requires mitering a 2 x 4 for the back, inner roof and floor, a carpenter's method that's straightforward to cut on the table saw or chop saw, or with a handsaw, but beyond the capacity of most jigsaws. If you like the sturdiness of this construction, but haven't acquired the knack of toe-nailing thick wood, you can use galvanized screws.

Whichever version you choose to build, mount the house on a metal pole using U-bolts. The angled sides and roof of this design blend easily into the natural landscape, and many people prefer it for that reason.

The extended back of the Peterson style birdhouse U-bolts directly to a smooth metal pipe. This is a good production design for populating fencerows and country fields with bluebirds.

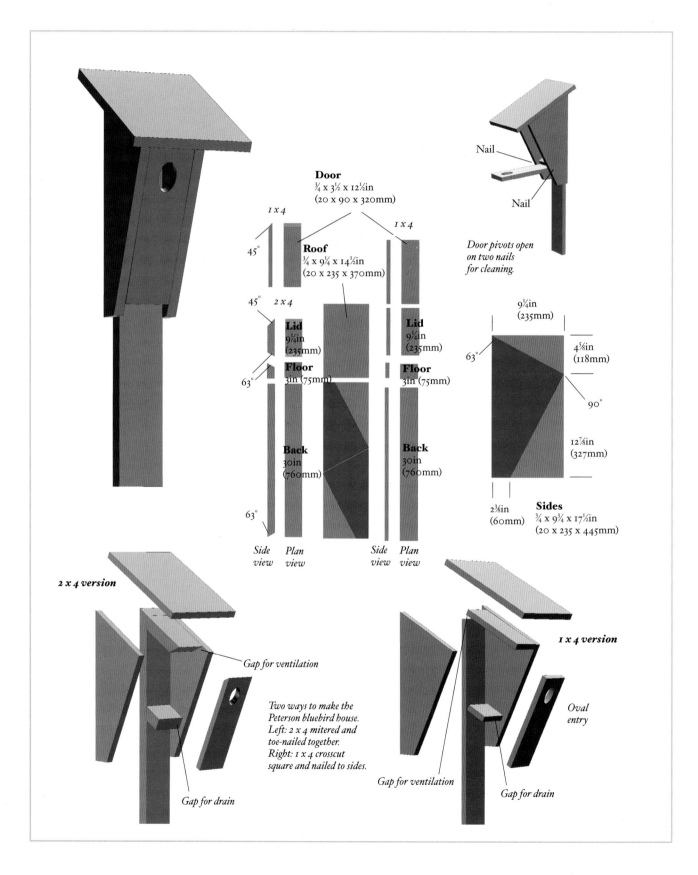

Door
¾ x 3½ x 12½in
(20 x 90 x 320mm)

1 x 4

45°

Roof
¾ x 9¼ x 14½in
(20 x 235 x 370mm)

1 x 4

Nail

Nail

*Door pivots open
on two nails
for cleaning.*

45° *2 x 4*

Lid
9¼in
(235mm)

Lid
9¼in
(235mm)

9¼in
(235mm)

63°

Floor
3in (75mm)

Floor
3in (75mm)

63°

4⅝in
(118mm)

90°

Back
30in
(760mm)

Back
30in
(760mm)

12⅞in
(327mm)

63°

2⅜in
(60mm)

Sides
¾ x 9¾ x 17½in
(20 x 235 x 445mm)

*Side
view*

*Plan
view*

*Side
view*

*Plan
view*

2 x 4 version

Gap for ventilation

*Two ways to make the
Peterson bluebird house.
Left: 2 x 4 mitered and
toe-nailed together.
Right: 1 x 4 crosscut
square and nailed to sides.*

Gap for drain

1 x 4 version

*Oval
entry*

Gap for ventilation

Gap for drain

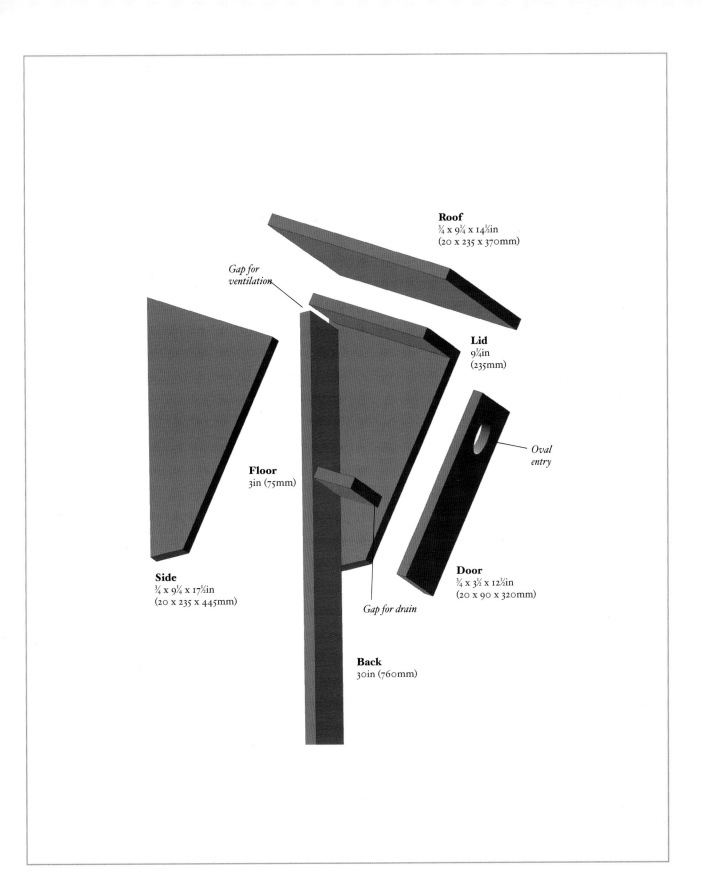

Roof
¾ x 9¼ x 14½in
(20 x 235 x 370mm)

Gap for ventilation

Lid
9¼in
(235mm)

Oval entry

Floor
3in (75mm)

Side
¾ x 9¼ x 17½in
(20 x 235 x 445mm)

Door
¾ x 3½ x 12½in
(20 x 90 x 320mm)

Gap for drain

Back
30in (760mm)

1

Cut all the parts. The photos show the 1 x 4 version because it is easier to build than the 2 x 4 version. Begin by nailing one side of the house to the lid piece. Align the wood at the side's 90-degree corner; it will fall short of the back edge.

2

Clamp the back to the side, leaving a ventilation gap between it and the lid piece. When you figure the pieces are in about the right place, nail it tight.

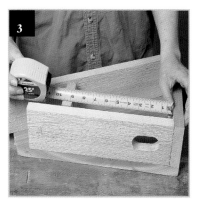

3 & 4

Set the door in position, flush with the edge of the side piece, so you can see where to locate the floor. Leave a small vent gap at the top of the door, and a drain gap where the floor meets the door. The tape shows more or less where it goes. Clamp the floor to the side, flip the box, and nail through.

5

The box closes in and becomes a sturdy house when you nail the second side onto the back, lid, and floor.

6

Now put the door back in position and experiment with opening it until you can see where the pivot point should be. Start the first nail, and make sure the door will open without jamming on the floor or back. Then transfer the nail location to the other side of the house, and drive both nails.

7

Saw or rout a water-shedding groove across the underside of the roof, about 1in (25mm) from the high edge. Locate the roof on the house so water dripping off this groove will run down the outside, not inside.

8 & 9

One way to lock the door is to insert a bolt or nail through a hole in the roof. Drill the clearance hole through the roof and into the top edge of the door. The speed square helps keep the drill lined up. Mount the birdhouse on a metal post using U-bolts.

Nuthatch chalet

Here is a cute little chalet suitable for nuthatches, chickadees, titmice, and other small songbirds. It is very quick and easy to build, and its roof makes good use of standard cedar shingles.

For drainage, cut the bottom a little smaller than the sides so there is a gap along one or both edges. Alternatively, if you would rather make the top corner of the bottom align exactly with the side, create drainage by drilling several ¼inch (6mm) drainage holes.

One of the roof shingles is nailed tight to the ends and floor, while the other is held in place by two brass screws. If you prefer a hinged opening, use barn shakes instead of shingles. They are uniform in thickness and meaty enough to receive hinge screws and small screw eyes.

The prism-shaped nuthatch chalet has only five pieces of wood instead of the usual six or more. It is very cute, and it couldn't be simpler to make.

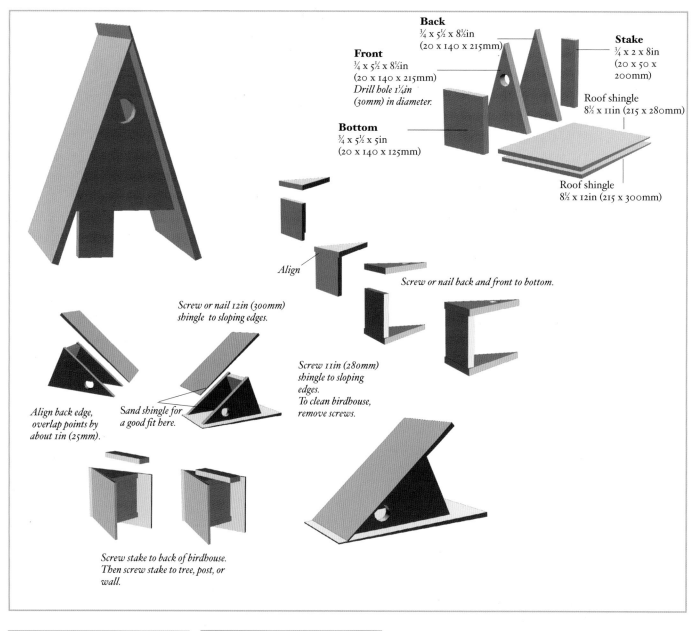

Back
¾ x 5½ x 8½in
(20 x 140 x 215mm)

Stake
¾ x 2 x 8in
(20 x 50 x 200mm)

Front
¾ x 5½ x 8½in
(20 x 140 x 215mm)
Drill hole 1¼in (30mm) in diameter.

Roof shingle
8½ x 11in (215 x 280mm)

Bottom
¾ x 5½ x 5in
(20 x 140 x 125mm)

Roof shingle
8½ x 12in (215 x 300mm)

Align

Screw or nail back and front to bottom.

Screw or nail 12in (300mm) shingle to sloping edges.

Screw 11in (280mm) shingle to sloping edges.
To clean birdhouse, remove screws.

Align back edge, overlap points by about 1in (25mm).

Sand shingle for a good fit here.

Screw stake to back of birdhouse. Then screw stake to tree, post, or wall.

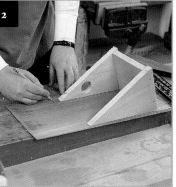

1
Cut all the parts. Nail the front and back of the chalet to the floor. Use 2in (50mm) galvanized siding nails.

2
Place the house body on the first roof shingle with the thick end down. Line up the back of the house with the edge of the shingle, leaving an overhang at the front. Mark the length to the peak of the front.

3

You can saw the shingle to length, or you can cut it with a knife. Use the speed square to guide the knife and make a cut across one side of the shingle. Flip the shingle over and make a second cut in the same place on the other side.

4

With the knife line on the edge of the workbench, snap the overhanging shingle down sharply. It will make a clean break at the knife line.

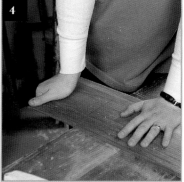

5

Sand the birdhouse lightly to remove rough edges. Use 100-grit sandpaper wrapped around a hard rubber block.

6

Rain is certain to enter, so even the smallest birdhouse has to drain. Drill several ¼in (6mm) drainage holes in the floor of the house.

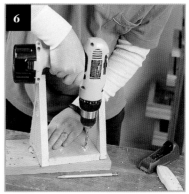

7

Position the first roof piece the same way you set it up, with the top edge meeting the peaks, and the back edges flush. Fasten the roof to the house with 1¼in (30mm) galvanized shingle nails

8

Position the second roof so the tip of the shingle extends a jaunty 1in (25mm) above the house peak. Fasten the second roof piece to the house body with two brass screws, which will be easy to remove when it is time to clean out the old nest.

9 & 10

Screw the mounting stake to the back of the birdhouse. Use 1¼in (30mm) galvanized screws. Now you can screw or nail the birdhouse to a tree, post, or wall.

Box birdhouse

Here is another traditional birdhouse design with a hinged lid for cleaning access. Keep the lid closed with a wire twist-tie through a pair of screw eyes, or with a guarded hook-and-eye that raccoons can't open. For additional protection against predators, extend the overhanging roof and sides from 2in (50mm), as shown here, to 4in or 5in (100mm or 125mm), and double the wood thickness around the entry hole.

A box like this is very suitable to being resized so it suits almost any kind of bird or critter. To make it big enough for barn owls and wood ducks, use plywood or T-111 grooved siding.

Squirrels, who otherwise are likely to enlarge the opening to suit themselves, will move happily into this style of box, though they seem to prefer the entry to be on the side instead of up front.

Make the entry 3in (75mm) in diameter, and scale the house so the bottom is a square roughly 9in (225mm) on each side. Giving squirrels their own houses encourages peaceful coexistence.

The box design scales easily to accommodate different species, including squirrels. Doubling the dimensions given in the drawing makes it about right for wood ducks. The green reeds were painted using a stencil cut from self-sticking plastic shelf liner.

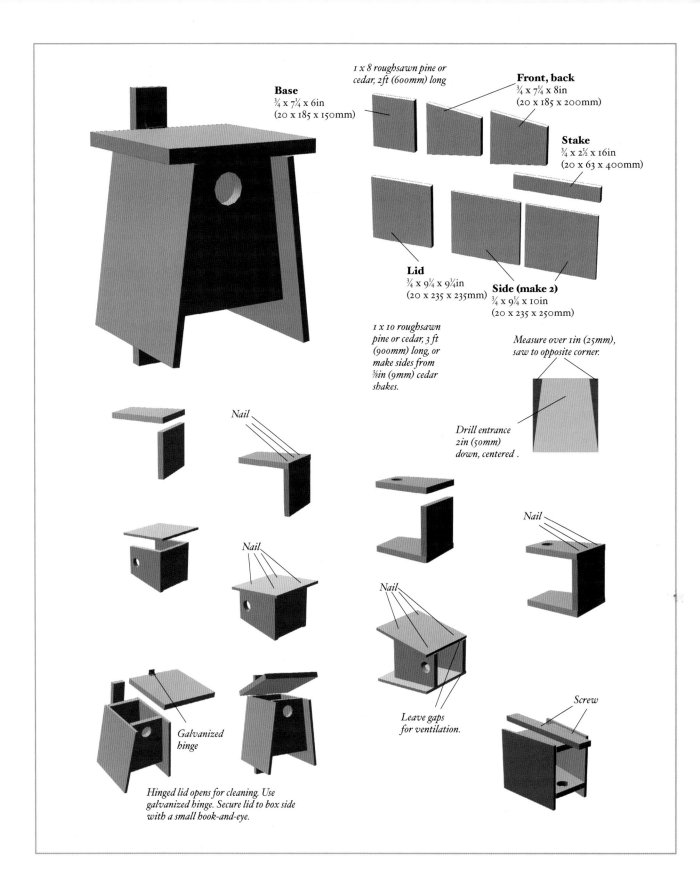

Base
¾ x 7¼ x 6in
(20 x 185 x 150mm)

1 x 8 roughsawn pine or cedar, 2ft (600mm) long

Front, back
¾ x 7¼ x 8in
(20 x 185 x 200mm)

Stake
¾ x 2½ x 16in
(20 x 63 x 400mm)

Lid
¾ x 9¼ x 9¼in
(20 x 235 x 235mm)

Side (make 2)
¾ x 9¼ x 10in
(20 x 235 x 250mm)

1 x 10 roughsawn pine or cedar, 3 ft (900mm) long, or make sides from ⅜in (9mm) cedar shakes.

Measure over 1in (25mm), saw to opposite corner.

Drill entrance 2in (50mm) down, centered .

Nail

Nail

Nail

Nail

Leave gaps for ventilation.

Screw

Galvanized hinge

Hinged lid opens for cleaning. Use galvanized hinge. Secure lid to box side with a small hook-and-eye.

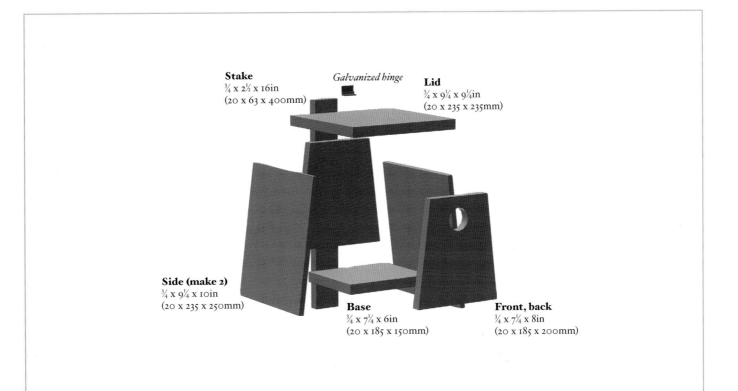

Stake
¾ x 2½ x 16in
(20 x 63 x 400mm)

Galvanized hinge

Lid
¾ x 9¼ x 9¼in
(20 x 235 x 235mm)

Side (make 2)
¾ x 9¼ x 10in
(20 x 235 x 250mm)

Base
¾ x 7¼ x 6in
(20 x 185 x 150mm)

Front, back
¾ x 7¼ x 8in
(20 x 185 x 200mm)

1 & 2
The front and back of the birdhouse are trapezoids—rectangles that taper from bottom to top. The slope is 1 in 8. To lay out the shape, start with square wood and measure over 1in (25mm) from both top corners. Connect these points with the bottom corners.

3
Clamp the workpiece on the bench with the layout line overhanging the edge, and steer the jigsaw along it. This is a very easy cut to make on the table saw or chop saw, with a miter angle between 7 and 8 degrees.

4
The precise angle doesn't matter so much as having a front and back that match. That is why you lay out and saw one piece, then trace it onto the other one.

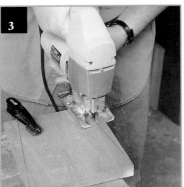

5
Clamp the birdhouse front onto a piece of scrap wood and drill the bird entry, (see chart in Birdhouse Woodworking section for size according to species). Here an expansion bit in a hand-brace is used, but you could use a hole saw or the jigsaw with a narrow blade started with a smaller drilled hole.

6
Set the front in position against the bottom. There should be a small drainage gap where the top edge of the bottom piece meets the sloping front piece.

7, 8, & 9
For a neat job, it is always best to make a layout line where the nails will go. Start the nails with the work-piece flat on the bench, then position the two pieces and drive the first nail. Check their alignment before proceeding with the second or third nails.

10 & 11
Saw cedar barn shakes to length and width for the bird-house sides, and nail them in place. The sides do not quite come up to the top of the front and back pieces (see II). The gap here is for ventilation.

12

Screw the mounting stake onto the back of the bird-house. Note that it must extend above the walls, because it is also the anchor for the hinged roof.

13

Attach the roof to the birdhouse with a single galvanized hinge. Screw the hinge to the roof piece first, then fasten it to the mounting stake.

14

If you made the hinge a tight fit with the roof closed, it probably will bind when you open it. The inside corner of the roof needs a little bit of clearance, so dub it off with 100-grit sandpaper.

15 & 16

Use the awl to start and twist a pair of screw eyes into the underside of the roof and the adjacent side.

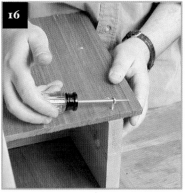

17

To keep the birdhouse roof closed against weather and predators, wire the two screw eyes together. Here a short piece of galvanized iron wire is used but you could use a trash-bag twist-tie too.

18

The mounting stake can be screwed directly to a tree, post, or building. Or it can be equipped with a pair of galvanized U-bolts for fastening to a smooth metal pole.

Plug birdhouse

Woodpeckers seem to like a tall box such as this, and the rougher the wood, the better. The best type of wood to use is log-sawn cedar fencing, rough sawn flat on one side with the bark left on the other side.

This project shows how to make a square box using any standard width of lumber. In other birdhouse projects, both sides overlap the front, resulting in a rectangular section. Here the sides are screwed or nailed together pinwheel fashion. This assembly pattern results in a square-sectioned box whose inside dimension is the width of the wood minus its own thickness.

Be sure to drill holes in the sides for ventilation, as well as in the bottom for drainage. If you can saw accurately, you can make the plug lid tight enough to stay put without mechanical assistance. Otherwise, add a removable screw, or pairs of eye-screws wired together, to hold it down. Either mount the birdhouse atop a pole or attach it to a tree trunk.

To attract woodpeckers, this blocky birdhouse should be mounted on the edge of a clearing in the woods.

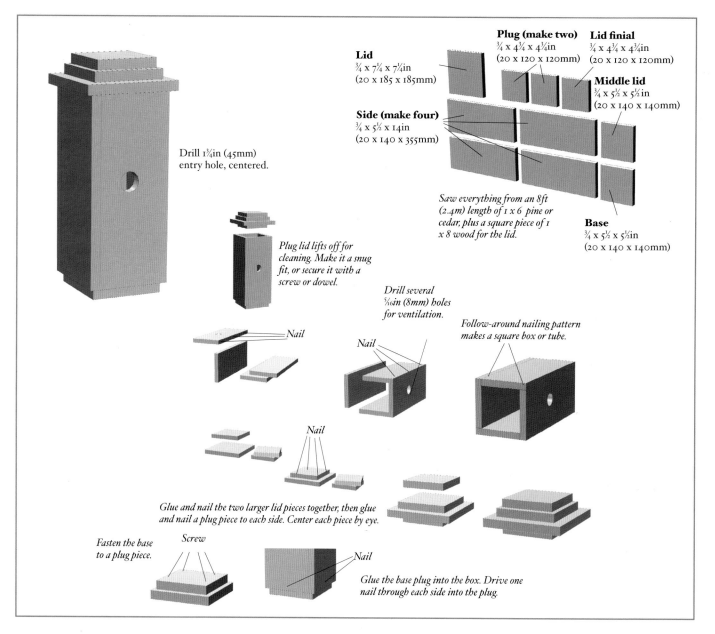

Drill 1¾in (45mm) entry hole, centered.

Lid
¾ x 7¼ x 7¼in
(20 x 185 x 185mm)

Plug (make two)
¾ x 4¾ x 4¾in
(20 x 120 x 120mm)

Lid finial
¾ x 4¾ x 4¾in
(20 x 120 x 120mm)

Middle lid
¾ x 5½ x 5½in
(20 x 140 x 140mm)

Side (make four)
¾ x 5½ x 14in
(20 x 140 x 355mm)

Saw everything from an 8ft (2.4m) length of 1 x 6 pine or cedar, plus a square piece of 1 x 8 wood for the lid.

Base
¾ x 5½ x 5½in
(20 x 140 x 140mm)

Plug lid lifts off for cleaning. Make it a snug fit, or secure it with a screw or dowel.

Drill several ⁵⁄₁₆in (8mm) holes for ventilation.

Follow-around nailing pattern makes a square box or tube.

Nail

Nail

Nail

Glue and nail the two larger lid pieces together, then glue and nail a plug piece to each side. Center each piece by eye.

Fasten the base to a plug piece.

Screw

Nail

Glue the base plug into the box. Drive one nail through each side into the plug.

1 & 2

Skilled people will just nail pieces together, but if you are learning you will find layout lines a big help. Likewise, it is much easier to start the nails with the workpiece flat on the bench.

3

To make a box like this reasonably watertight, glue the seams with an outdoor-rated, gap-filling glue. This is yellow type II carpentry glue. With very rough wood, use silicon house caulk or bathtub caulk, but let it cure for a week before you put the house up.

4

The first corner is the trickiest, but you can take most of the wobble out of it by propping the top piece on an as-yet unused piece of wood.

5

This end-view shows the pinwheel assembly pattern. When used with equal-width wood, this pattern results in a square box or tube. The more usual box pattern, as in the basic birdhouse, results in a rectangular tube where one side is wider than the other by twice the wood thickness.

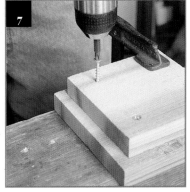

6

The expansion bit in a standard brace allows you to drill any size hole. Make the hole to suit the species you hope to attract.

7

Adjust the fit of the plug pieces before you fasten the lid and base assemblies together. In soft cedar like this, you can clamp the assembly to the bench and drive the screws directly into the wood, without having to drill clearance holes or pilot holes.

8

Drill ⁵⁄₁₆in (8mm) or ³⁄₈in (9mm) holes near the top of the birdhouse, for ventilation. Drill several holes into the base, so any stray water will drain.

9

Attach the birdhouse to a suitable post or tree.

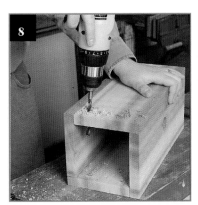

Hexagon feeder

No birdhouse book would be complete without a feeder. This one is hexagonal, a six-sided shape that is surprisingly easy to make. It is designed to hang by light chains from a tree branch or an overhanging eave. You recharge it through the hole in the top piece, then plug it with the cap.

Most people remember from school how to construct a hexagon with a ruler and compass. You use the compass to draw a circle, then without changing the compass setting, step it around the outside of the circle. The result will be six equally spaced points which, when connected, reveal the hexagon.

The key to making the feeder is drawing a hexagon whose staved sides match the width of your wood. Simply set the compass to the width of the stave, draw the circle, and step the six points around it. Your friends will think you are a math whiz, when all you had to do was not adjust the compass.

The green leaves and purple flowers were painted onto bare wood using stencils cut from self-sticking vinyl shelf liner. Craft shops sell a low-cost swivel knife, which makes it easy to cut flowing shapes.

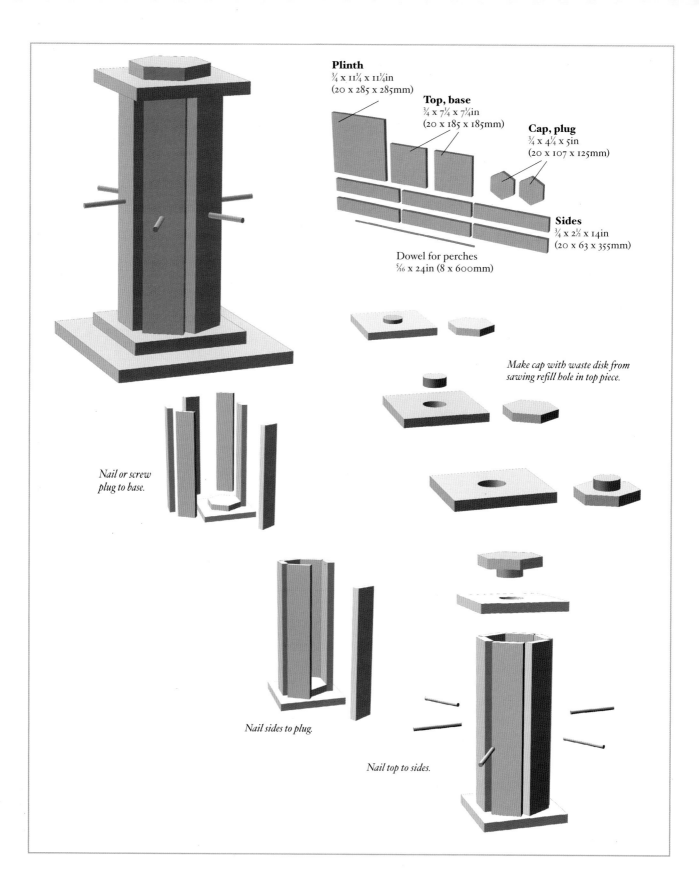

Plinth
¾ x 11¼ x 11¼in
(20 x 285 x 285mm)

Top, base
¾ x 7¼ x 7¼in
(20 x 185 x 185mm)

Cap, plug
¾ x 4¼ x 5in
(20 x 107 x 125mm)

Sides
¾ x 2½ x 14in
(20 x 63 x 355mm)

Dowel for perches
⁵⁄₁₆ x 24in (8 x 600mm)

Make cap with waste disk from sawing refill hole in top piece.

Nail or screw plug to base.

Nail sides to plug.

Nail top to sides.

I

Cut the parts. Set a pencil compass to the width of a side piece. This distance is the side of the hexagon you need to draw.

2 & 3

Lines connecting the corners of the wood will cross at the center. Set the compass on this point and draw a circle on the wood.

4 & 5

Without changing its setting, step the compass around the circle drawn on the wood. The sides of the feeder should match the points you just marked on the circle.

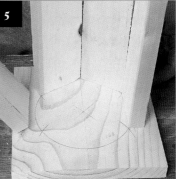

6

Connect the points on the circle. The sides of a hexagon meet at an angle of 120 degrees. Extending the lines to the edges of the workpiece will help you aim the jigsaw.

7

Clamp the workpiece to the bench and jigsaw the sides of the hexagon. Be sure to clamp so the sawing line overhangs the edge of the bench.

8

Screw the hexagonal plug piece to the base using three 1¼in (30mm) screws. This wood is western pine, which tends to split, so a pilot hole was drilled for each screw.

9

Use two galvanized siding nails to fasten the first side to the base piece. Use the second hexagon, which will become the lid, to support the side for nailing.

10

It is a little too tight to set the nail with the hammer, so use a small nailset to tap the head of each nail down flush with the surface of the wood.

11 & 12

Use a hole saw to cut the opening in the top piece. Clamp the workpiece atop a block of scrap on the bench. The hole saw cuts a neat disk, which you must pry out of the saw.

13

Center the scrap disk on the cap piece. Hold it there with a dab of glue and a screw driven through the center hole left by the saw.

14, 15, & 16

With the top piece flat on the bench, turn the feeder upside down and set it in position. Draw around it, then turn the whole assembly upright so you can nail the top piece to the ends of the six side pieces. Use galvanized siding nails.

17

Drill four ⅜in (9mm) holes in the valleys between each pair of sides. The birds peck the seeds through these holes. You might have to clean up any splintered wood with the tip of a small knife.

18

Drill holes in the center of each side for the perches, and glue the short sections of dowel in place.

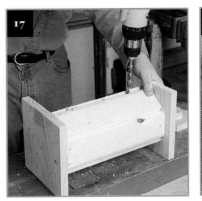

Twin gable bird box

The twin gable house not only looks very nice, it also meets the criteria for a bird-friendly dwelling. The recessed corners, along with the intersecting roofs, make it look a lot more complicated than it actually is. Size the house according to the chart in the Birdhouse Woodworking section, to suit the bird species you hope to attract.

Most of the birdhouses in this book are held together by nailing each side to the adjacent one. However, the sides of this birdhouse are nailed to the floor, not to each other. Because the wood is rough, and also because nailing is never 100 percent precise, there will be gaps in the corners, providing both ventilation and drainage.

Because the bottom is structural, it is not removable for cleaning. Instead one side opens with a galvanized hinge and one of the roof gables opens right along with it.

The gable roof is made out of 18in (450mm) hand-split red cedar barn shakes, which are about ½in (12mm) thick, with a rough surface. Note that there is a difference equal to the thickness of a cedar shake between the height of the birdhouse front and back, and the two side walls. This allows the long roof pieces to tuck underneath the short gables. With this birdhouse project, you do not have to measure or calculate any roof angles. The gable ends and roof pieces are all created from direct measurement.

Paint really changes the look of these shake-roofed birdhouses. Do not paint inside the entry hole or any part of the interior.

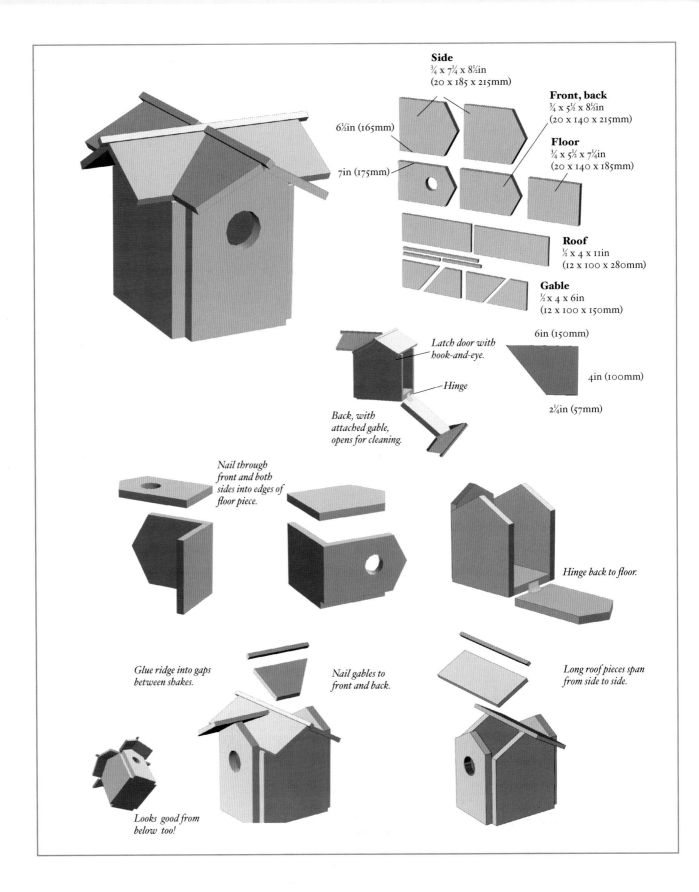

Side
¾ x 7¼ x 8½in
(20 x 185 x 215mm)

Front, back
¾ x 5½ x 8½in
(20 x 140 x 215mm)

6½in (165mm)

Floor
¾ x 5½ x 7¼in
(20 x 140 x 185mm)

7in (175mm)

Roof
½ x 4 x 11in
(12 x 100 x 280mm)

Gable
½ x 4 x 6in
(12 x 100 x 150mm)

Latch door with hook-and-eye.

6in (150mm)

Hinge

4in (100mm)

Back, with attached gable, opens for cleaning.

2¼in (57mm)

Nail through front and both sides into edges of floor piece.

Hinge back to floor.

Glue ridge into gaps between shakes.

Nail gables to front and back.

Long roof pieces span from side to side.

Looks good from below too!

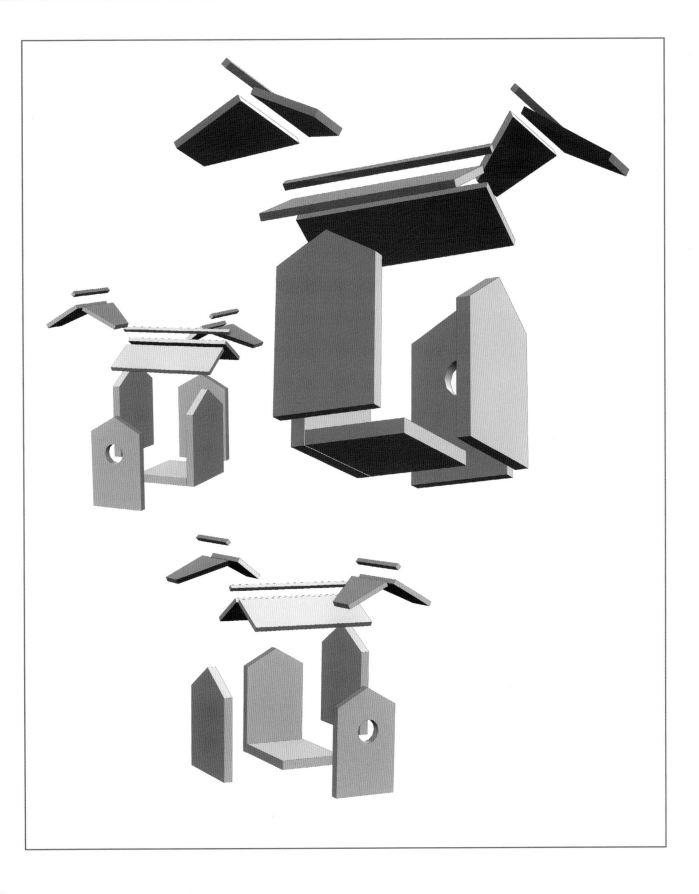

1

Cut all the parts. Fasten the front and sides to the floor piece with 2in (50mm) galvanized siding nails. Nail through the wall pieces into the edge of the floor piece.

2 & 3

The back of the birdhouse is the cleanout door. Fasten it to the bottom with a single galvanized hinge. You need to do it now because the back has to be in position before you can fit the roof.

4

The long roof pieces span from side to side. Use 1¼in (30mm) galvanized shingle nails to fasten them to the sides of the birdhouse. It does not matter if there is a gap at the peak, because the ridge pieces will fill it in.

5, 6, & 7

A pair of hook-and-eye latches keeps the birdhouse door closed. Screw the hook-side eye into the door of the birdhouse. Then use it to locate the mating screw eye on the side wall of the birdhouse. Use an awl to make a starter hole, and also to get some leverage on the screw eyes as you twist them home.

8

Follow the measurements on the drawing to lay out the gable pieces. Here hand-split red cedar barn shakes are used for roofing material. The shakes are about ½in (12mm) thick.

9 & 10

Cut the gable on the layout line. Use any fine saw, such as the Japanese dozuki saw shown here, or else clamp the wood to the bench and use a jigsaw. For safety's sake, wear safety glasses or a face shield whenever the sawdust is flying.

11

Fit each gable piece in position. It will help if you measure and mark the center of the long roof pieces, and bring the gable point up to it. There will be some wiggle room, so go for what looks best to you. (See sidebar on page 116 for advice on how to get the gable measurements right.)

12 & 13

To make the ridge pieces, split square sticks off a barn shake. This material is easy to split with a knife, though you might have to tap the knife into the wood to get it started. The shake sides were sawn, so your first split probably won't make a straight stick. Once you have made a split edge, subsequent splits will run straight.

14

Squeeze a little outdoor-type carpentry glue onto the ridge piece. You could also use silicone caulk instead, but not regular white aliphatic resin glue, since this is not waterproof.

15 & 16

Use strips of masking tape to clamp each ridge piece in position while the glue dries. If you would like a little more insurance, tap a small brass pin through the ridge piece into the side or end of the birdhouse. When complete, attach the birdhouse to a suitable post.

Getting the gables right

1

If you changed the angles atop the sides and ends of the birdhouse, the gable measurements on the drawing won't be right. The first step in laying out the gable roof is to mark the center of the main roof, by connecting the peaks at front and back. This is where the point of the gable roof will end.

2

Use a piece of roof material to find the point on the birdhouse eave where the gable angle or valley should end. Hold the roof material on the birdhouse end and mark its width at the eave.

3

The valley formed by the gable roof falls on the line connecting the ridge center to the eave point—the two points you marked in the previous two steps. Measure the distance between these two points. This distance is the length of the angled side of the gable roof.

4

Set the ruler on one corner of the roof material and swing it until the valley measurement found in the previous step intersects the opposite edge. Draw this diagonal line, then saw the material on the line.

5

Hold the newly sawn gable piece in position on the birdhouse. It should sit flat on the end wall, and fit neatly against the long roof piece. Mark the overhang you want and saw to length.

6

All four gable pieces are the same. Now that you have made one piece that fits, trace around it to make the other three.

Tall martin house

Purple martins, which eat incredible quantities of insects, like to congregate in colonies. The traditional martin house is like an apartment block, with space for six or eight martin pairs in each layer. However, martins will also occupy a cluster of high-rise towers like this one. Each tower houses three martin pairs. It is good to make them two at a time. You can mount the towers on a common base atop a single pole, or on more than one pole set close together.

This design evolved from the twin gable house and shares many of its virtues. Rough wood and sloppy nailing guarantee gaps at the corners, taking care of ventilation and drainage. One whole side opens for cleaning. While you could make the opening side hinge, it is simplest to fasten it in place with two or three brass screws. And like the twin gable house, the opening side carries a piece of the roof along with it.

This good-looking apartment house has false eaves that make it seem to be more complicated than it really is. Hopefully it will attract a group of bug-eating purple martins.

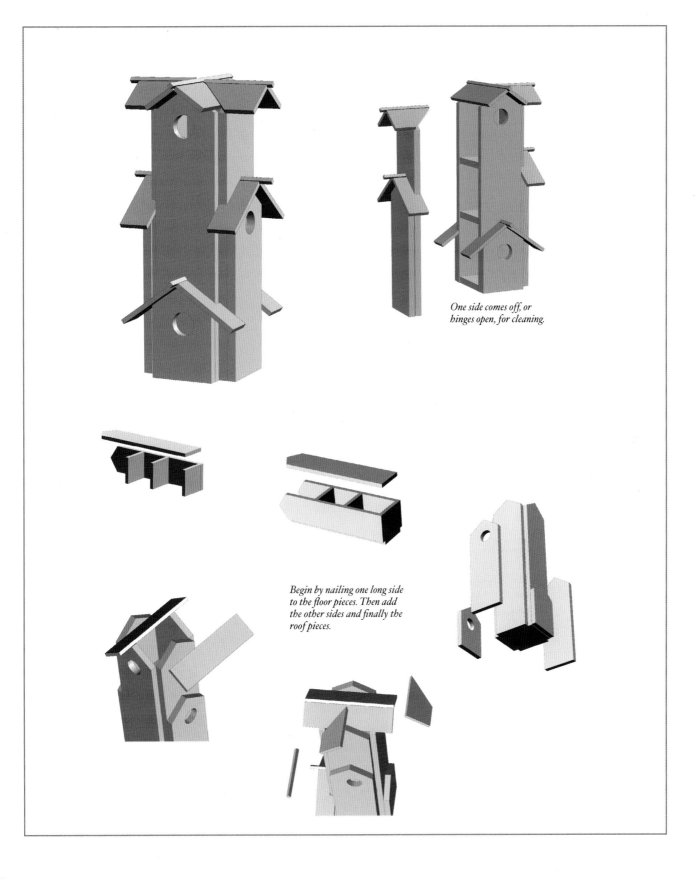

One side comes off, or hinges open, for cleaning.

Begin by nailing one long side to the floor pieces. Then add the other sides and finally the roof pieces.

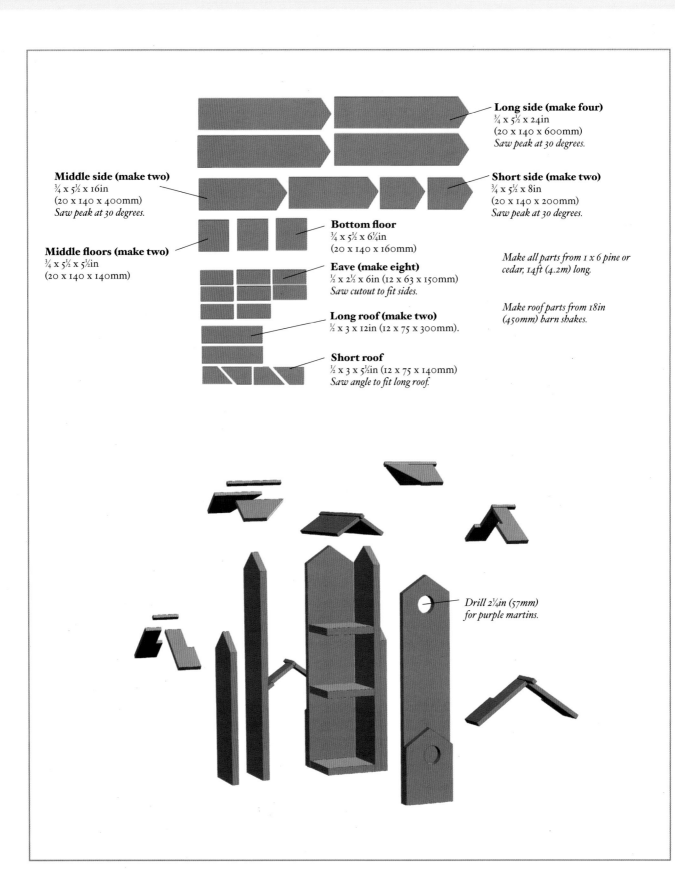

Long side (make four)
¾ x 5½ x 24in
(20 x 140 x 600mm)
Saw peak at 30 degrees.

Middle side (make two)
¾ x 5½ x 16in
(20 x 140 x 400mm)
Saw peak at 30 degrees.

Short side (make two)
¾ x 5½ x 8in
(20 x 140 x 200mm)
Saw peak at 30 degrees.

Bottom floor
¾ x 5½ x 6¼in
(20 x 140 x 160mm)

Middle floors (make two)
¾ x 5½ x 5½in
(20 x 140 x 140mm)

*Make all parts from 1 x 6 pine or
cedar, 14ft (4.2m) long.*

Eave (make eight)
½ x 2½ x 6in (12 x 63 x 150mm)
Saw cutout to fit sides.

*Make roof parts from 18in
(450mm) barn shakes.*

Long roof (make two)
½ x 3 x 12in (12 x 75 x 300mm).

Short roof
½ x 3 x 5½in (12 x 75 x 140mm)
Saw angle to fit long roof.

*Drill 2¼in (57mm)
for purple martins.*

1

Cut all the parts. The height of the tall birdhouse is somewhat arbitrary; this one is 24in (600mm). Use one side for the layout and divide the height into three, and mark the location of the floor pieces on it. To avoid potential confusion square the thickness of the floor pieces across the inside face of the layout side.

2

Use the speed square to extend the layout marks onto the edges of the layout piece. You will be able to see these marks even after the house is closed in.

3

The layout marks will guide you in starting two nails for each floor piece. Start the nails with the wood flat on the bench, then block it up so you can drive the first pair of nails into the bottom floor piece.

4

The bottom floor piece projects beyond the side by ¾in (20mm), that is, by the thickness of the wood. This gives the opening side a platform on which to rest, making it easier to remove for cleaning and reclosing it in the field. However you must also remember to saw one long side ¾in (20 mm) short to compensate.

5 & 6

After you have nailed the layout side to all three floor pieces, use the speed square to align and nail one of the adjacent sides. Here a fourth floor piece has been added—an interior ceiling for the top house—which is optional. With the second long side nailed in place, the construction will stabilize and it will be quite easy to locate and attach the third long side.

7

The middle side pieces give the birdhouse visual interest and create the line of the eaves. They are simply nailed to the long sides using 1½in (37mm) nails, which won't protrude on the inside. Attach the short side piece in the same way.

8

If you chose to extend the floor, saw the remaining long side short by the floor's thickness and nail the one remaining short side piece to it so the two together form a lip. This subassembly is the opening side, which should be screwed in place now.

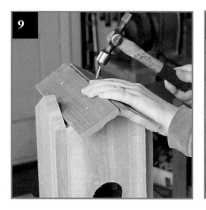

9

Center the long roof pieces across the birdhouse and nail them in place. Be sure they span the fixed sides, not the opening side.

10

Hold one of the short roof pieces up to the long roof to mark where the angled cut begins and ends. This procedure is detailed in the twin gable house (page 116). You might have to make a couple of test pieces before you get it right.

11 & 12

Use a small, fine saw to cut the angle on the short roof piece. Hold it in place to check the fit, and if necessary, saw it again. When you get one piece to fit right, use it as a template to make three more.

13

The eave pieces contribute a lot to the look of the birdhouse, but they have to be cut to fit. Hold the first piece in place to find where it intersects the side, mark the cut and extend the angle across the edge of the piece.

14

Stand the eave piece up on edge to saw the angled cut. Saw ¾in (20mm) into the wood—that is, the thickness of the side pieces—and stop.

15

Tap the knife into the wood to split the waste piece off the eave. You could saw this line if you prefer, but splitting the soft cedar shakes is quick and easy.

16, 17, & 18

Check the fit of the eave piece and if you like it, nail it in place. If the fit is not quite right, you'll probably be able to fix it by whittling with the knife, or by sanding, or by making a new piece.

19, 20, & 21

Make some long, square sticks for ridge pieces by splitting a straight-grained cedar barn shake. Tap the knife into the end of the wood, then twist it as you work it down into the wood.

22 & 23

Spread water-resistant outdoor glue on two adjacent sides of each ridge piece and fit it into the spaces between roof pieces and eave pieces. Use masking tape to hold the ridge in position while the glue dries. When complete attach to a suitable mounting post.

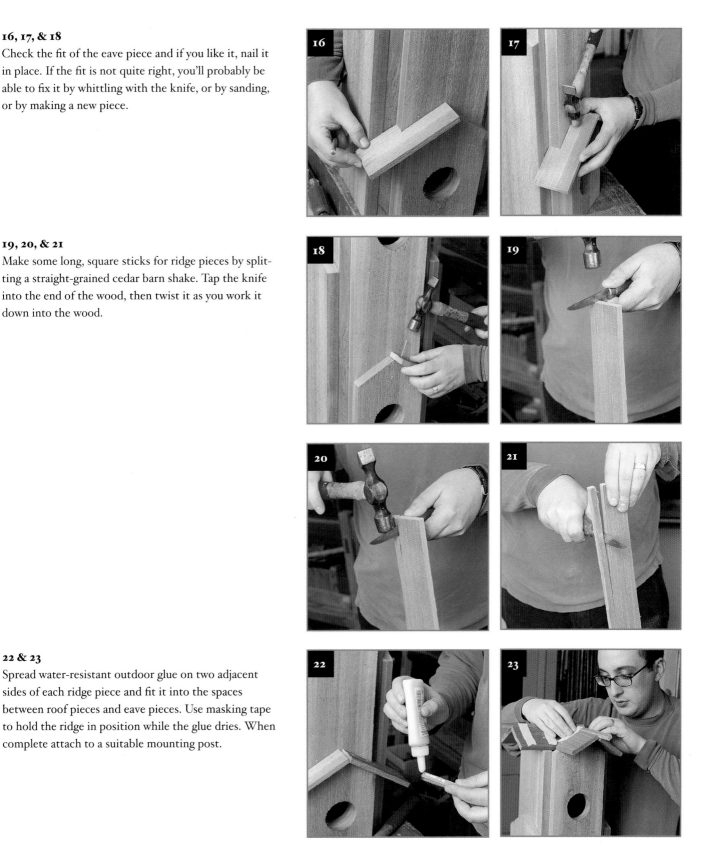

Modern birdhouse

The roof of this birdhouse pivots open for cleaning and for observing the nestlings inside. Your mother probably told you the parent birds wouldn't return if you touched the nest, but bird experts now say that's wrong and it's harmless. So, if you can mount the box where you can get at it, and succeed in luring birds to nest in it, you can just lift the lid whenever you want to watch the show.

The design comes from an inspirational series of birdhouse drawings published a few years ago by the architect Malcolm Wells. He argued that all the birdhouses you might ever need can be made from scrap and found lumber, at little or no cost. Consequently his designs emphasize visual style over the economical use of materials.

The following steps show how to lay out the rounded top of the roof's pivot ears, and how to locate the hole centers for drilling in advance of assembly. None of this is especially critical—you can get workable results if you eyeball the curve or trace it around a small varnish can, fit the pivoting roof in place, and drill the bolt holes through the sides and ears at once. Just be sure to get the holes in the same relative place in both sides, so the roof pivots easily. This version has a level floor. You could take the design a step further by making the floor slope the same as the roof.

This version of the modern birdhouse is meant to be mounted on the side of a building, for species that prefer this location, such as robins and barn swallows.

The rough sawn cedar birdhouse will weather to match the worn shingled siding on this country home.

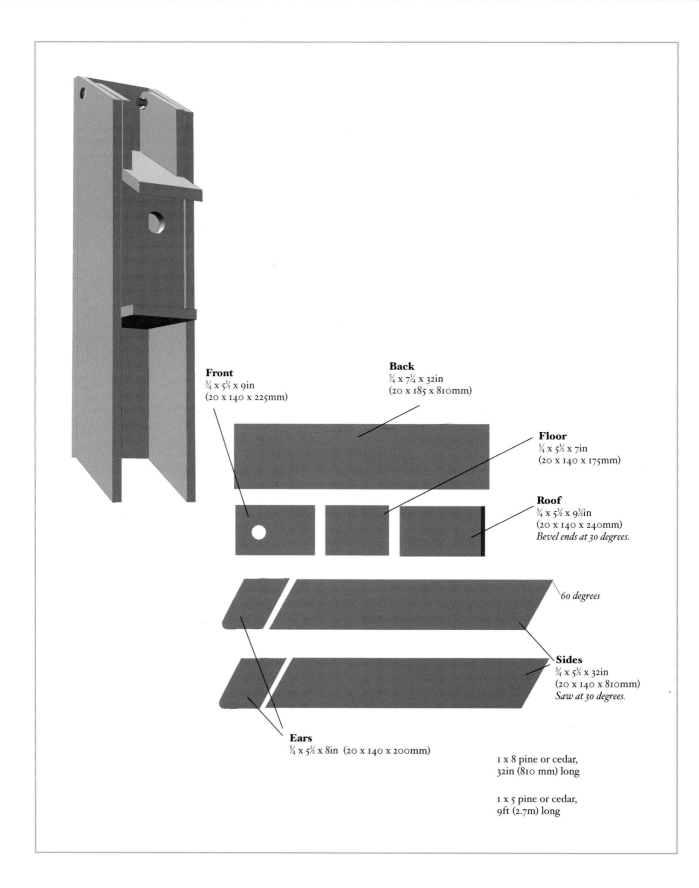

Front
¾ x 5½ x 9in
(20 x 140 x 225mm)

Back
¾ x 7¼ x 32in
(20 x 185 x 810mm)

Floor
¾ x 5½ x 7in
(20 x 140 x 175mm)

Roof
¾ x 5½ x 9½in
(20 x 140 x 240mm)
Bevel ends at 30 degrees.

60 degrees

Sides
¾ x 5½ x 32in
(20 x 140 x 810mm)
Saw at 30 degrees.

Ears
¾ x 5½ x 8in (20 x 140 x 200mm)

1 x 8 pine or cedar,
32in (810 mm) long

1 x 5 pine or cedar,
9ft (2.7m) long

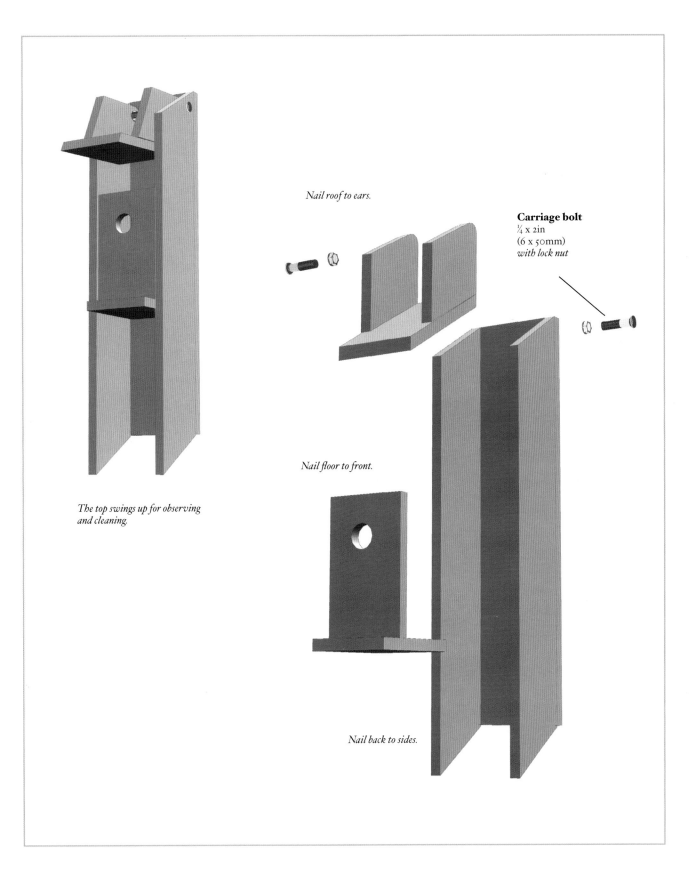

The top swings up for observing and cleaning.

Nail roof to ears.

Carriage bolt
¼ x 2in
(6 x 50mm)
with lock nut

Nail floor to front.

Nail back to sides.

1 & 2

Cut all the parts, then clamp and nail the birdhouse sides to the back piece. Use 2½in (60mm) galvanized nails. If your wood is rough on only one side, turn the rough side in so the fledglings will have something to cling to. The finished result is a U-shaped trough with sloping ends.

3

Drill an entry hole gauged to the species you wish to attract in the front piece (see chart in Birdhouse Woodworking section). Then drill a second hole in a small scrap of wood and nail it to the front, to make a double thickness at the entry. This discourages cats and raccoons from reaching inside for their morning eggs.

4 & 5

Saw a 30-degree bevel on both ends of the roof piece. Most jigsaws can make a bevel cut if you tilt the sole of the saw, but don't trust the dinky little scale you might find engraved on the trunnion. Check the angle with a protractor or drafting triangle.

6

You'll probably be able to make the ear pieces using the scrap from sawing the sides. The problem is how to locate the hole for the pivot bolt, and lay out the curved end that permits the ear to pivot. You could eyeball it, but if you want to get it right the first time, please follow our sequence. To begin, set a compass to about 2in (50mm) and with its point on one corner of the wood, draw an arc from edge to edge.

7

With the compass at the same setting, set the point on the ends of the arc where it meets the edge of the wood and draw two intersecting arcs. These arcs intersect at the midpoint of the angle.

8

Set the speed square on the corner of the wood and on the point where the two arcs intersect, and draw the line. This line bisects the angle

9

Place the compass point where the bisector crosses the first arc you drew. This is the pivot point. Set the compass to the distance from the pivot point to the edge of the wood. Draw an arc. This is the line you will saw to round the tip of the ear piece.

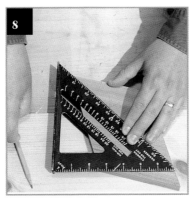

10

Clamp the two ear pieces together, with the layout piece uppermost. Use the speed square to help you drill a ¼in (6mm) hole down through both pieces of wood.

11

Clamp an ear piece to each side piece, and use the existing hole to guide you in drilling a matching hole through the side piece.

12

Clamp the ear piece so it extends off the edge of the workbench, and steer the jigsaw around the curve you drew. If the curve comes out a little bit rough, you might want to sand it smooth.

13

Stand the two ear pieces on the bench and position the roof piece on top of them. Note that the beveled end of the roof piece merges smoothly with the angled side of the ear, and that the round end of the ears is down and away. Draw layout lines for the nails that will join these parts with a pencil.

14

With the roof piece flat on the bench, start two nails on each layout line. Use 2½in (63mm) galvanized siding nails.

15

Now reassemble the roof piece and the two ears so you can nail them together. Check how they line up with your fingers and take the time to get it right.

16

Drive the nails through the roof piece into the ear pieces. Here the birdhouse is being made outdoors on a temporary bench set up on sawhorses (as detailed in the Birdhouse Woodworking section).

17

Slip the roof assembly into position and hold it with the two carriage bolts. Check to make sure it pivots easily, and if it hangs up anywhere, find the problem and correct it. Don't run the lock nuts down tight just yet, because you might yet want to take it all apart to fiddle.

18

With the roof closed, hold the front of the birdhouse in position and mark where it will go. Leave a little ventilation gap between the front and the roof. You'll also be able to fit and mark where the floor should attach to the front, leaving a small gap for drainage and ventilation at the floor's back edge.

19

Clamp the birdhouse front to the floor piece and attach them together with nails.

20

Put the front-floor subassembly in position between the birdhouse sides. Check all your ventilation and drainage gaps, and use little shims of scrap wood to keep them the size you want. Clamp across the sides to hold everything in position for nailing.

21

Nail through the birdhouse sides into the front and floor. Drive two 2½ in (63mm) galvanized siding nails into each piece. Flip the birdhouse over and do the same from the other side.

22 & 23

See how nicely the birdhouse opens for viewing and cleaning? Now tighten the lock nuts so the raccoons can't open it by themselves, and if you want to be sure about that, drill a hole through the side and into the ear for a locking pin. Finally, attach the birdhouse to a suitable place on the side of a building.

Martin apartments

Here is a traditional apartment house for bug-eating purple martins, made in a non-traditional way. Martins prefer their houses to be 15ft (4.5m) to 20ft (6m) in the air. Most martin houses consist of interlocking pieces of plywood with a lot of grooves and precise joints that have to be jiggled into place. The resulting house is heavy and ungainly, tedious to make, and quite difficult to mount on top of a high pole.

This martin house attempts to solve these problems. It may seem like it has a lot of parts, but it is entirely modular in design—there are a lot of parts, but only a few are different. It can be assembled atop a wooden or a metal pole, manageable piece by manageable piece. And it is just as easy to disassemble for cleaning.

The house shown here rests on blocks screwed to a wooden pole. In hurricane country, it would be prudent to screw or bolt the hollow central column to the post, through the rafter connectors.

The drawings show a roof made of ⅜in (9mm) plywood or some other sheet material. In the steps western red cedar shingles were used and you could also use barn shakes, or any convenient sheet material that's available to you. If you plan to paint the house, the traditional color is white, which reflects some of the sun's heat.

Easy-to-clean modules make up this colony dwelling for purple martins. It is painted to match the trim on the house nearby. The doodads are wooden beads from the craft shop, fastened with siding nails.

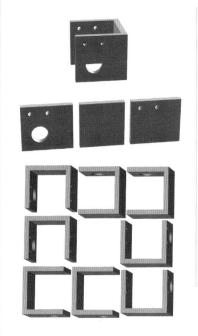

Drill the bird entry about 1in (25mm) up from the bottom. Offset all the holes by the thickness of the wood, so they'll be centered once you assemble the module.

Be sure to assemble all the modules the same way around. That way eight identical three-sided units will fit neatly together.

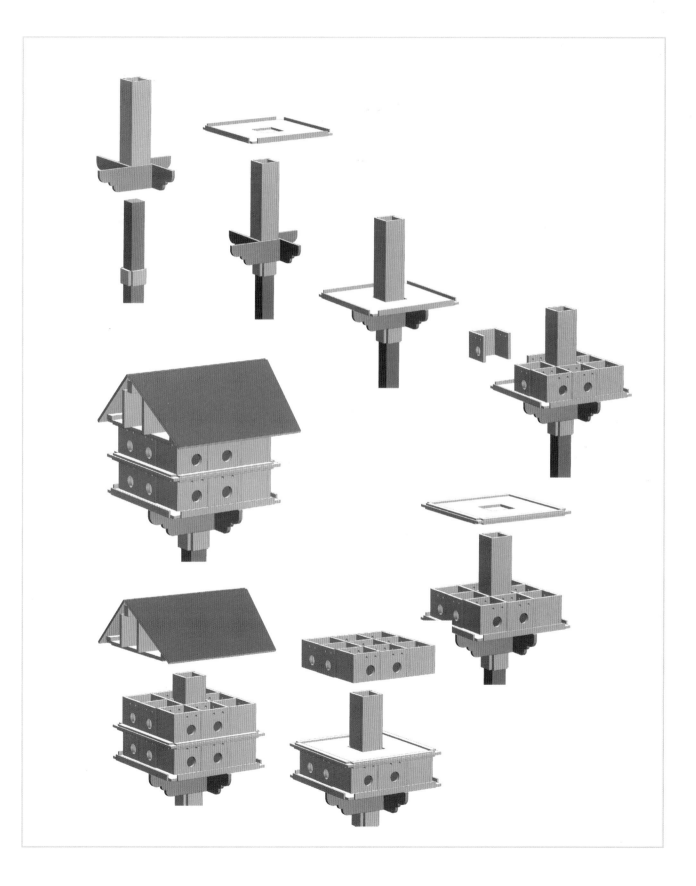

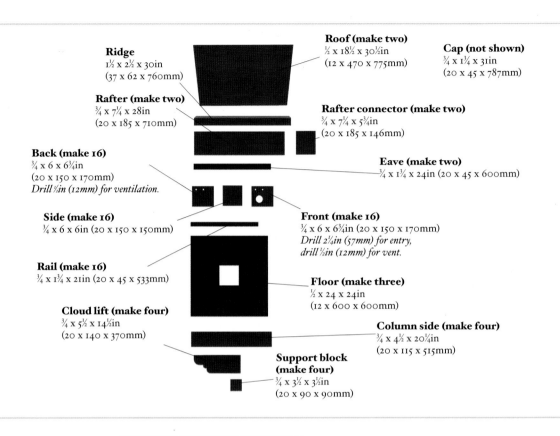

Ridge
1½ x 2½ x 30in
(37 x 62 x 760mm)

Rafter (make two)
¾ x 7¼ x 28in
(20 x 185 x 710mm)

Back (make 16)
¾ x 6 x 6¾in
(20 x 150 x 170mm)
Drill ½in (12mm) for ventilation.

Side (make 16)
¾ x 6 x 6in (20 x 150 x 150mm)

Rail (make 16)
¾ x 1¾ x 21in (20 x 45 x 533mm)

Cloud lift (make four)
¾ x 5½ x 14½in
(20 x 140 x 370mm)

Roof (make two)
½ x 18½ x 30½in
(12 x 470 x 775mm)

Cap (not shown)
¾ x 1¾ x 31in
(20 x 45 x 787mm)

Rafter connector (make two)
¾ x 7¼ x 5¾in
(20 x 185 x 146mm)

Eave (make two)
¾ x 1¾ x 24in (20 x 45 x 600mm)

Front (make 16)
¾ x 6 x 6¾in (20 x 150 x 170mm)
*Drill 2¼in (57mm) for entry,
drill ½in (12mm) for vent.*

Floor (make three)
½ x 24 x 24in
(12 x 600 x 600mm)

Column side (make four)
¾ x 4½ x 20¼in
(20 x 115 x 515mm)

**Support block
(make four)**
¾ x 3½ x 3½in
(20 x 90 x 90mm)

1

Use the holesaw to drill the bird entrances in all 16 front pieces. Clamp each workpiece to a protective piece of wood atop the workbench. A large holesaw like this generates a lot of torque—grip the drill with both hands, and tuck it into your body. A face shield or goggles are essential to protect the eyes from flying debris.

2

Pry the waste plug out of the hole saw with a screwdriver—that's what the slots in the saw are for. If you drill most of the way through from one side and then flip the workpiece over to complete the hole, the waste piece won't get so far into the saw and it will be easier to eject.

3

Change to a ½in (12mm) bit and drill the two ventilation holes in each front and back piece. The hole is small so the drill is easier to control, but it is still essential to clamp the workpiece to the bench.

4

Here is the stack of parts for one layer of martin apartments, and the first three-sided house assembled. As you can see in the drawings, these units become complete compartments when they are fitted together, the side of one becoming the back of the next.

5

In this design, the front and back pieces overlap the side piece, so you nail through them into the side piece. It is possible to assemble these same parts right-handed or left-handed, but important to make them all the same way around. Keep the first one nearby and use it for reference for the other houses.

6, 7, & 8

Start the nails with the workpiece flat on the bench, then hold it in position to drive the nails home. Align the parts with your fingers. If something shifts, you will feel it before you see it.

9
The column fits over a square post, so its interior should also be square. Since it is made of four parts that are the same width, it has to be assembled pinwheel fashion. Use nails to tack the parts in place, then make it strong with 2in (50mm) screws.

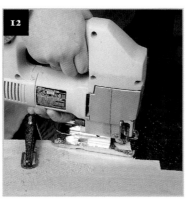

10
The cloud lifts connect the lower floor of the martin house to the central column, and stabilize the whole construction. The cloud shape is arbitrary, but if you do decide to use it, make a paper pattern to trace on the four identical parts.

11 & 12
You can't just saw a curve like this cloud shape, because the saw will get stuck in the corners. First, saw straight in from the edges to each inside corner, thus removing most of the waste wood. Now it is easy to complete the shape without the saw getting stuck.

13
The cloud lift stabilizes the whole assembly, so it is important to make it square to the central column. Draw layout lines all the way around.

14
Use water-resistant outdoor glue, and roll it on both surfaces where the cloud piece fits onto the column. A disposable trim-painting roller does the best job of spreading glue.

15

Clamp each cloud lift to the central column, tap it into exactly the right position, then drill pilot holes and anchor it with four 2½in (63mm) screws. Note that the cloud lifts follow one another around the column pin-wheel fashion, just like the column parts themselves, with the back end of each piece exactly flush with the column side.

16 & 17

All three floor pieces need a centered square hole a little larger than the central column. Drill a ½in (12mm) starter hole in one corner of the square. The hole allows you to start the jigsaw. Saw straight to the two adjacent corners, then saw curves toward the opposite corner.

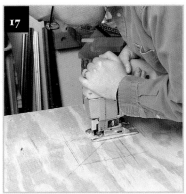

18

Put the first floor piece over the central column. A loose fit is better because the house needs a lot of ventilation.

19

Assemble eight of the martin apartments onto the first floor (see the drawing). There will be two bird openings on each side and one blank wall. Center the assembly on the floor plate, and draw a layout line around the apartments to locate the rail pieces. Add the middle floor piece and the rest of the apartments and draw more layout lines.

20 & 21

The rail pieces on the first floor stand up on edge and are fastened to the edges of the plywood. Roll glue onto each edge of the plywood and nail the rail pieces to it. The rail pieces stop short of the corners, not only for looks but also to make sure rain water can't get trapped.

22 & 23

The eight middle floor rail pieces locate and retain the apartments on the floor above and below. The layout lines you made in the test assembly step ensures that you leave enough room for the apartments. Roll glue on each rail piece, clamp them to both sides of the plywood floor, and fasten them in position with ¾in (20mm) galvanized screws.

24 & 25

The top plate provides the structure for the roof. It has two eave pieces glued and screwed to it. These pieces have to be thicker than the rail pieces because you will be nailing the roof itself to them.

26 & 27

The two rafter pieces, and the rafter connectors, make a box around the hole in the top plate. Make sure the opening is a little larger than the sawn hole in the plywood, clamp the parts in position, and screw them securely together as well as to the plywood plate.

28

The ridge piece, which is beveled on its top edges, is centered on the rafter connectors and screwed securely to them. Note that the ridge piece is longer than the rafters and eaves and that the eave pieces, the long rafter pieces, and the ridge piece all run in the same direction.

29

While it is simple to make a roof out of ¼in (6mm) plywood, you could use three courses of cedar shingles in two layers as shown here. The birdhouse doesn't need this much roof, but it does look good. Divide the distance from ridge to eave in three to find the shingle overlap. Draw layout lines so you know exactly where to nail into the ridge, rafter, and eave pieces. Use 1¼in (30mm) galvanized shingle nails.

30

A little shape makes the roof look really good. Draw a line from the end of the ridge down to the end of the eave piece, and jigsaw the shingles along this line. You would shape a plywood roof in exactly the same way.

31

There is a gap at the peak of the roof, so cut a straight piece of wood to cover it and nail it in place.

32

Drop the lower floor onto the central mast, and arrange eight of the bird apartments on it. Make sure they are all the same way around and right-side up. The retainers fastened to the middle floor trap the apartments in place.

33

The second layout of apartments goes on exactly the same as the first. Once you get one apartment in the right position, there's only one way to fit the rest.

34

When you drop the roof into position, the retainer strips glued to it will trap the second layer of bird apartments. You can reach in through the end gables to screw or bolt the roof to the central mast, locking the whole assembly together. Attach the birdhouse to a suitable wooden post, either atop blocks or by bolting the central column to the post.